LEARNING FOR THE COMMON GOOD

LIBERAL EDUCATION, CIVIC EDUCATION, AND TEACHING ABOUT PHILANTHROPY

THOMAS JEAVONS
Associate Director of Programs
Association of American Colleges

Foreword by
ROBERT L. PAYTON
Director
Indiana University Center on Philanthropy

ASSOCIATION OF AMERICAN COLLEGES, 1991

THIS WORK WAS SUPPORTED BY
THE AMERICAN ASSOCIATION OF
FUNDRAISING COUNSEL
TRUST FOR PHILANTHROPY,
THE CARNEGIE CORPORATION OF NEW YORK,
THE EXXON EDUCATION FOUNDATION,
THE HEARST FOUNDATION,
THE LILLY ENDOWMENT, INC.,
AND
THE W.K. KELLOGG FOUNDATION

Cover: Classical column arrangement
and ornamentation (detail);
from *The Complete Encyclopedia of Illustration*

Published by
Association of American Colleges
1818 R Street, NW
Washington, D.C. 20009

Copyright 1991

ISBN 0-911696-52-0
Library of Congress Catalog No. 91-74017

CONTENTS

FOREWORD

This book should become an underground classic. It is part of the growing *samizdat* of protest literature against the hegemony of specialization that has dominated higher education for thirty years. The vehicle is the study of good works; the strategies include engagement with ideas and their consequences, testing theory against practice. It is all unabashedly value-laden and normative yet self-critical, seeking to be ethically concerned and disinterested at the same time.

This book contains a report, but more than anything else it is an essay on liberal education. Liberal education is the loom that weaves together the development of mind and the development of character. The distinguished historian Karl Weintraub once told a class entering the College of the University of Chicago that the first objective of a liberal education is to come to some understanding of *the complexity of things*. Trying to grasp the way good works happen, trying to understand one's own as well as others' participation or abstention from service, means becoming immersed in the complexities of society, individual, and culture.

It happens that the study of "philanthropy" is an exceedingly effective form of liberal education. This book examines the ways in which faculty members and students have developed courses and tested them over time, learning about learning as well as about the tradition of voluntary action for the public good.

The ideal of liberal education stubbornly persists despite its failures, just as democracy does. To mention "citizenship" and "public service" is to begin to make the connection between philanthropy and democracy, an issue of some urgency in other parts of the world (most especially today in Central and Eastern Europe). A certain kind of education—liberal education—is more effective in preserving and advancing the ideals of freedom and democracy than other, more utilitarian, educational models.

These ideas are subversive not only to the idolatry of specialization but to the self-serving form of professionalism that has corrupted the modern university. To bring the study of philanthropy into the university is to call attention to the mission of a university—a higher and more socially responsible mission than recent media reports would suggest. The study of philanthropy well may result in new efforts at institutional reform—efforts that are more timely than ever and reforms that are long overdue.

Liberal education insists that philanthropic ideas be weighed and reflected upon, discussed and evaluated. The study of philanthropy must include the principal critiques of voluntary action. Philanthropy brings out the tension between individual and collective responsibility, the age-old debate about *desert*, the underside of voluntary association represented by the Ku Klux Klan or ethnic conflict.

What the author advances as politically sensitive and sophisticated about inclusiveness I will challenge as merely fashionable. Those are precisely the kinds of differences that need to be made visible and subject to discussion as part of liberal education and that grow naturally out of voluntary efforts in behalf of the well-being of others.

What must be avoided is the easy politicization of the subject—leading to charges, whether well-grounded or not, of a politically correct agenda among the advocates of philanthropic studies. Fortunately, almost every field of philanthropic activity generates diverse points of view, and it is easy—even unavoidable in some cases—to find alternative perspectives and values that must be considered.

Whether new courses need to be developed to introduce these issues or to provide new ways of focusing on them is an open question. At my institution, we are trying as hard to encourage the modification of existing courses as we are to encourage the development of new ones. In some cases, courses need no more than a few additional or substituted questions or topics, some changes in the reading list, some different ideas for papers that are based on experience

as well as reading. We hope that the questions of good works will come to permeate the curriculum rather than be appropriated as the private domain of a given profession or discipline. It is also an argument against subordinating the study of philanthropy to philosophy or ethics—even though there is a good case for saying that is where it most clearly belongs.

That is one more reason why "nonprofit management" should not become the dominant model for study. The study of philanthropy must be grounded in the liberal arts. Otherwise it soon will come to be a field of practice without roots, as so many of the professions are. Philanthropy as voluntary action then could become primarily dependent on other fields for examination of the underlying assumptions on which practice is thought to be based. Social work began as "philanthropy" a century ago; it moved quickly to practice, leaving theory behind in sociology. The modern study of philanthropy should pay attention to that lesson.

There are, as the author points out in quoting professor Susan Ostrander of Tufts, different reasons for teaching philanthropy. Dr. Ostrander finds that the study of philanthropy is useful to the study of sociology. There also are different reasons for people to become involved in philanthropy as volunteers; students often give refreshingly frank statements about what they're looking for when they sign up for the course or seek out a community service opportunity. Altruism and idealism are not always the most important motivators.

The popular version of the philanthropy course as a capstone course probably is a good idea. Such a course may have a direct effect on students' choices of graduate and professional work or employment. The capstone course can be a bridge among disciplines and educational experiences and also a bridge between the campus and one's career. It is a timely moment for most students to reflect on where they're going as well as on where they've been, and on what their values are.

Most of us perceive an important change in student values, a more thoughtful assessment of what the good life is and how one might seek it. Whether good works are seen as central to a career or to the good life, a challenging senior-year course is the best time to raise these questions.

Having said that, it would seem equally important that other courses be modified so that basic knowledge about the place of voluntary action in American life becomes part of the ordinary content of courses in American history, politics, and economics. The capstone course should not be the first time that philanthropy enters the student's consciousness. More students should come to the capstone course already having wrestled with the critique that comes from collective choice theory, the place of philanthropy in social movements, or the differences among interest groups.

As someone who teaches philanthropy and is captivated by the complexity of it, I find this book to be helpful, practical, suggestive, occasionally but gently opinionated, and worth circulating on every campus.

ROBERT L. PAYTON
Indiana University
Center on Philanthropy
June 1991

INTRODUCTION

Sometimes, when things go just right, one has the experience of undertaking a project to address one particular issue or need and then discovering that the work being done creates opportunities to address other issues or solve other problems. At the Association of American Colleges, that has happened a number of times in recent years. The AAC/AAFRC Program on Studying Philanthropy, which ran from 1986 through 1991, is one example of a combination of purposeful effort and fortuitous circumstances.

The practices of organized philanthropy and voluntary association have played a large and crucial role in shaping the character of the economic, political, and social life of American society—a role unparalleled in any other society. In no other developed nation have voluntary association and private philanthropic initiative had such a central and substantial function in supporting and shaping the society's cultural life, in meeting human needs, and in exploring new ways to address human and social problems. Yet it has been and still is true that the vast majority of graduates of our colleges and universities know virtually nothing about these traditions of philanthropy and voluntarism and their functions in the civic, social, and economic order they are entering.[1] Indeed, most of these students are not even capable of defining the term "philanthropy."

If one of the obligations of American higher education is to help its students understand the history and character of their own culture, or at least of the society of which they will be a part, that seems unacceptable. In light of these circumstances, when representatives of the board of the American Association of Fund Raising Counsel (AAFRC) Trust for Philanthropy came to AAC with an idea for a project that might help broaden and deepen undergraduates' understanding of the history and functions of philanthropy in American culture, it seemed a worthwhile cause.

The long-range goals of the project were to draw more attention to this area of study and develop materials for teaching about it, so that the subjects of "philanthropy and voluntarism" might be included in courses in history, sociology, economics, political science, and other fields where they are so often and so inappropriately overlooked. In order to draw attention to this area of studies, however, it seemed necessary first to create whole courses about philanthropy that were academically sound and rigorous, intellectually challenging, and exciting to potential students. Therefore, the project provided grants for developing and offering pilot versions of such courses in the arts and sciences.

We now see this program as a clear success in terms of these limited initial goals. The courses that have been created are intellectually challenging, interesting to students, and appropriate and helpful additions to an undergraduate liberal arts curriculum. They have drawn attention to philanthropy as an area deserving more academic study and as a phenomenon that should be given more attention in a number of arts and sciences fields.

The great majority of the courses developed with the support of this program appear likely to become permanent parts of the curricula of their respective institutions, and some already have spawned related offerings. Finally, in a number of cases we find professors in the departments where these courses are offered thinking about how topics raised in these courses might be—even should be—worked into other courses.

Even more pleasing, though, are results we did not anticipate. The possibilities these courses hold for revitalizing other aspects of undergraduate education that need renewal and the insights they have generated about ways of enriching liberal arts courses are even more exciting than the success of the courses in and of themselves. Our experience with this program suggests:

☐ Courses about philanthropy and voluntarism may provide especially valuable and appropriate vehicles for

the work of "civic education," renewing the once prominent emphasis on preparation for citizenship (and, in some measure, "values education") in liberal education.

☐ Including elements of experiential education in liberal arts courses not only helps students better understand the particular subject matter; it also improves the development of students' intellectual capacities, which should be among the essential outcomes of higher education.

☐ Courses about philanthropy and voluntarism provide an intellectual basis for, and crucial forum for reflection on, the experiences of community service in which so many students now are engaged and which so many colleges now are urging upon their students.[2] Institutions of higher education are missing an extraordinary opportunity for enriching their students' learning if they do not create curricular structures that provide occasions for thinking critically about and reflecting on those experiences.

This monograph has two purposes. One is simply to report on the curriculum development program AAC has run for the last five years, which supported the creation and implementation of undergraduate liberal arts courses about philanthropy. The other is to reflect on what we have learned from this program about the potential value of such courses: the ways such courses can be vehicles for renewing attention to the work of civic education in colleges and universities and improving the quality of undergraduate education more generally.

Obviously, the latter aspect of this agenda is larger and more ambitious than the former. Accordingly, it will receive more space and energy. We want to consider carefully and thoroughly the justifications for adding another area of studies to the undergraduate curriculum before we describe the particulars of our experiment in doing that.

Frankly, we do not presume that the reader of this document will agree that philanthropy is a subject meriting attention in and of itself. We believe it is. Just as importantly, however, courses about philanthropy and voluntarism also can meet the larger and most significant purposes of college education.

We begin with three basic premises. The first is that, for the most part, American institutions of higher education in recent years have not given enough attention to their responsibilities for preparing young people for the activities and obligations of citizenship in a free and self-governing society. The second is that this is unfortunate, to say the least. In these times, to set aside this aspect of the tradition of the *artes liberales* in higher education is to fail to

develop in younger people (and the body politic) a set of skills and understandings that they cannot do without if they are to preserve, lead, and extend a healthy, just, and free society. The third premise is that this situation can be remedied, and some of the remedies available are not only congruent with but actually can enhance the other aspects and goals of higher education that faculty members and administrators most value.

We will argue more fully for the importance of including courses and exercises in the educational experience of undergraduates that help them see and understand—and even practice—the responsibilities of citizenship. In fact, the fundamental intellectual and personal capacities we must develop in students as part of a meaningful civic education are virtually identical with intellectual and personal capacities that should be among the essential outcomes of any truly liberal education.[3] Thus, efforts to reinvigorate the tradition of civic education within liberal education, at a time when that is much needed, also may be immensely useful in developing essential intellectual abilities of students more broadly and even in deepening their understanding of the methods and content of particular disciplines.

We will discuss specifically how courses within the realm of the liberal arts about philanthropy and voluntarism can serve all of these purposes. We will look at examples of the ways the courses in AAC's Program on Studying Philanthropy were designed and implemented and examine how students were affected by them.

We then will look more specifically at AAC's project, giving a little of its history and describing briefly each of the courses and their most prominent strengths and weaknesses. We also will talk briefly about key elements and dynamics that many of the courses had in common and how those elements and dynamics were experienced by the students and campuses that participated in the program. We will look, too, at how the institutions benefited from that participation in their particular environments.

Finally, we will consider which aspects of these courses seemed most successful and least successful. This discussion will set the framework for a few recommendations we will make for others who are interested in developing similar courses. Here we will consider especially questions of context—that is, how to fit the content, structure, and pedagogy of different courses to particular settings so that these elements will be most fruitful. For example, the questions of whether to include an experiential component in a course, how to inte-

grate that experience with the traditional academic components, and how to develop the connections to and supports for fieldwork (if included) are questions whose answers depend in great measure on the environment in which the course is being offered—the kind of college or university, the kind of community in which it exists, the kinds of students who attend it.

We also will have a few suggestions deriving from our experience with this project with more far-reaching implications for improving the quality of liberal education.

The appendices include materials from AAC's Program on Studying Philanthropy, as well as some other sources, which we think will be of value to those interested in teaching about philanthropy and voluntarism, in civic education at the postsecondary level, and in enriching liberal arts education by including experiential or fieldwork components.

While this monograph is a report on a curriculum development project which focused primarily on creating courses about philanthropy, it is intended to address a broader audience. We believe that, in addition to those interested in philanthropic studies, this document will be useful for anyone concerned with improving and enriching undergraduate education, especially those who think preparation for citizenship should be a part of that education. We put this volume forward in hopes of contributing to those efforts at improvement, and we look forward to being part of a continuing dialogue around these concerns.

As we offer the fruits of this work to the public, we must express our appreciation to a number of people and agencies who made it possible. First among these is the AAFRC Trust for Philanthropy—especially the late Maurice Gurin, whose special commitment to this project was crucial to its success. John Chandler, AAC's President Emeritus, and Daphne Layton, former assistant director of programs at AAC, helped design it, raised the funds to support it, and got it established on a sound footing.

We also want to thank the members of the Project Advisory Committee, who played an essential role both in offering advice on the program's design and in helping select those who received the grants and developed the courses described here. The committee members were:
☐ Virginia A. Hodgkinson, Vice President for Research, Independent Sector
☐ Kathleen D. McCarthy, Professor, Center for the Study of Philanthropy, City University of New York Graduate School

☐ John G. Simon, Chairman, Yale Program on Nonprofit Organizations, Yale University
☐ John Van Til, Professor, Rutgers–The State University of New Jersey, Camden Campus
☐ Paul N. Ylvisaker, Professor, Graduate School of Education, Harvard University.

Obviously, none of this would have been possible without the generous support of the program's funders. These included, in addition to the AAFRC Trust for Philanthropy, the Carnegie Corporation of New York, the Exxon Education Foundation, the Hearst Foundation, the Lilly Endowment, Inc., and the W. K. Kellogg Foundation.

Finally, the most important participants in this project were the creative, energetic scholars and teachers who designed and offered these courses at their respective institutions. (A listing of the faculty participants and their courses is found in Appendix C.) Without their thoughtful and diligent efforts we would have none of the ideas, examples, and insights presented in the pages that follow. We hope this report fairly reflects the exceptional quality of the work they did in creating and offering their courses to their students.

PHILANTHROPY AND CITIZENSHIP

The philanthropic tradition in America long has been marked by a crucial and persistent tension. It is the tension between the compassionate, charitable impulse to give wherever there is suffering and need and the skeptical, cautionary voice that says such giving must be disciplined by careful analysis, study, and concern about creating dependency in the recipients of charity. It is the tension reflected in the remarks of John D. Rockfeller:

We must always remember that there is never enough money for the work of human uplift, and that there never can be. How vitally important, therefore, that the expenditure should go as far as possible, and be used with the greatest intelligence.[4]

In essence, the practice of philanthropy in this country has been at its best when it has been shaped by what could be called "a critical compassion"—that is, a genuine concern for and empathy with the condition of others melded with the capacity to see things objectively and in a broader perspective. Without the former, there would be no giving and volunteering at all, or at least not nearly as much as there is; without the latter, what giving and volunteering there is often would be misdirected, or at least much less effective than we would hope.

Thinking about the connections between the practice of philanthropy—the giving of one's time or money for the benefit of others or "the common good"—and the practice of citizenship more broadly, it seems apparent that this "critical compassion" is a prerequisite for both. The citizen must have a set of values that includes caring and respect for others as well as caring for "the common weal," or there is little likelihood that she or he will become constructively engaged in public life. Yet empathy and altruism without an informed perspective and the capacity for critical thinking ultimately are inadequate as a basis for constructive civic involvement.

Americans traditionally have expected higher education to help prepare students for citizenship

Americans traditionally have expected higher education to help prepare students for citizenship, cultivating in students both of the capacities just mentioned. They have expected, and many still do expect, that a college education—especially a liberal education—will do at least two things: give students a broader perspective and knowledge base while teaching them to think carefully and analytically; and encourage and reinforce the development of basic ethical values of integrity, tolerance, respect for others, and responsibility.

Higher education has come under attack in recent years for failing its students and society in both these respects. These attacks have not always been well-founded, but there can be no denying the gap between the expectations of the public (as well as the rhetoric of college catalogues about preparing students for citizenship) and the performance of colleges and universities in this realm.

Obviously, one's views of whether institutions of higher education truly are obligated to prepare their students for citizenship, and what it means to do so, are dependent on one's understanding of the whole educational enterprise. For those claiming to offer a liberal education, however, there is a tradition that can guide and challenge their perspectives and practices.

At its origins, liberal education—an education in the *artes liberales*—was conceived of as that kind of education particularly appropriate to the training and development of those who would shoulder the responsibilities of citizenship in a free society. The freedom for which this education prepared the student was of two kinds: first, political freedom, the freedom (and obligation) to participate in the process of governing society; second, the freedom of a leisured class to pursue knowledge or art for its own sake, the freedom to participate in the formation of culture.[5]

In the Greek city-state in which the ideals of liberal education first emerged, the class of citizens who enjoyed either of these freedoms, we must recognize, was quite restricted. That fact alone, however, cannot negate the value of this conception of education and its purpose. Indeed, in our increasingly complex world, the need to educate persons who can and will participate responsibly and creatively in the opportunities and obligations of citizenship has never been greater. Many of us would still affirm that the pursuit of these ideals of the *artes liberales* in higher education is essential to the development of such individuals. This tradition of liberal education—holding many variations and tensions within it—is one that we wish to continue to thrive, both for its inherent, personal value and for its social value.

As we consider whether our colleges and universities are effective in providing such a liberal education, however, it is important that we recognize some of the longstanding tensions within this tradition and the ways these tensions have shaped the enterprise, assumptions, and activities of higher education. Bruce Kimball argues that one of the key tensions within this tradition of liberal education is between a "philosophical" conception and a "rhetorical" one. He suggests that the balance and emphasis has shifted back and forth between these views—with first one and then the other dominating curricular and pedagogical design and practice over the centuries.

The philosophical conception gave preeminence to logic and literature in earlier times—and in more recent centuries has emphasized the sciences and humanities—as things to be studied for their own sake in the pursuit of truth and the advancement of knowledge. The rhetorical conception gave preeminence to grammar and rhetoric as training which enabled the citizen to participate in public debate and decision making; in this conception, the study of logic, the arts, and science provided the understanding and substance that should shape and inform those debates and decisions.

With the melding of the classical and Christian traditions, and later with the influence of the post-Enlightenment humanist tradition, an emphasis on instruction in ethics and the formation of virtue was added to this second conception. In the seventeenth and eighteenth centuries—in the aftermath of the Enlightenment—it was this view of liberal education, with a focus on the rhetorical arts and literature and on the inculcation of moral values, that held sway. In short, the primary focus was on preparing individuals to be virtuous citizens. This is the conception of liberal education that initially shaped the ideals and curricula of the liberal arts college in America.

If one looks at the mission statements of most colleges and universities in the United States today, one still sees evidence of these ideals. Indeed, as one observer has noted, this is a realm in which "rhetoric [has] waxed unrestrained, [but] these claims clash rudely with the reality."[6] Most institutions make some claim that one of the purposes or outcomes of the education they offer young people is encouraging their development as whole persons, including the formation of their character as well as their intellect. Not infrequently, those institutions also claim to prepare students to be better—that is, more responsible—citizens in a free society. It is apparent that one of the reasons institutions of higher education make these claims is that this is one of the outcomes our society expects. Beyond mentioning such ideals in their mission statements or catalogues, however, what is actually done in the curricula or programs of these institutions to address these purposes is highly questionable.[7]

Kimball notes that around the beginning of the twentieth century, "Many of the universities, encouraged by the advancement of pragmatism in ethical theory and by the scientific emphasis on value-free research, abandoned the idea of training the virtuous citizen."[8] A survey of the programs, curricula, and pedagogical approaches of most American colleges and universities in recent years certainly would confirm this judgment, despite what mission statements may say. What was largely abandoned then does not appear to have been recaptured since. Beginning with the assumption that this trend is not a good thing, AAC's project explored one possible avenue for redressing this situation.

CHAPTER TWO

◼

CIVIC EDUCATION AND LIBERAL EDUCATION

AN HISTORIC MISSION

PUBLIC EXPECTATIONS

CIVIC EDUCATION
AND LIBERAL EDUCATION

The classical ideal of education was focused on a public community purpose, namely good citizenship.... The humanists added to the goal of education for good citizenship the goal of education for self-fulfillment: they wanted citizens who were also good people.[9]

Why should American colleges and universities be concerned with education for citizenship or the development of civic consciousness in their students? There are several reasons. One is that these concerns have been a key part of their historical mission and should not be abandoned without strong justification. A second is

that this is a part of the public's expectation of collegiate education—an important part of the way colleges and universities serve the public good in exchange for their privileged status as tax-exempt institutions. A third reason—perhaps the most compelling—is that energy and attention spent on educating students for citizenship will enhance liberal education more generally. Indeed, one cannot offer a liberal education in any meaningful sense without educating for citizenship. As Elizabeth Minnich has said, "Without civic education what we offer is poor education."[10]

Taken together, these reasons provide a strong case for colleges and universities to refocus some of their energies on improving the preparation of their students for citizenship; this is a part of the educational agenda that colleges and universities should be pursuing more strongly. As we shall see, the curricula focusing on philanthropy and voluntarism developed in AAC's Program on Studying Philanthropy offer effective ways to do so.

AN HISTORIC MISSION

In her monograph *Renewing Civic Capacity*, Suzanne Morse observes:
Early colleges and universities were seen as unifiers for the goals of the larger society. They performed this role in three basic ways:
1) promoting a common American culture;
2) teaching moral philosophy within the institution that, among other purposes, was to integrate various disciplines and to serve as an ethical guide for students; and
3) producing leaders for America that were to be, in Jefferson's words, "an aristocracy of talent and virtue."[11]
Most American colleges and universities no longer can serve as unifying forces for our society in the first two ways just cited, even if

most could agree—which is by no means certain—that this is desirable. The first point is one of the contentious issues in today's battles over the curriculum, with the question of what is "a common American culture" being one on which we likely will find little or no agreement. And since the majority of four-year colleges in this country are either public institutions or explicitly secular institutions, the likelihood of "moral philosophy" making a comeback in the curriculum seems very slim. The last item on Morse's list, however, merits further consideration.

In the days of our early colleges and universities, the accepted views of what leadership was and who could be a leader were very narrow. Jefferson's use of the term "aristocracy" reflects the fact that, despite the establishment of a new democracy in this country, the prevailing views of leadership at that time were constricted and very hierarchical. Moreover, we know as well that only white males were admitted to those institutions that were to develop this "aristocracy of talent and virtue."

Now, however, our views of what leadership is and who can be a leader are much broader and more complex. Most prominent writers on the subject emphasize that genuine leadership is less a function of position in a hierarchy than it is a result of a person's ability to see things differently than her peers and act in a way that catalyzes their vision and engages their commitment to action. In this view, virtually everyone may have a leadership role to play—at different times and in differing contexts—in the life of his or her community.[12]

Considering the problems facing our various communities and our society at large, such leadership is desperately needed. It is vital that colleges and universities make much more concerted efforts to develop the aristocracy of talent and virtue of which Jefferson speaks, recognizing that this "aristocracy" now has to be much larger and far more inclusive than someone of Jefferson's time ever could imagine. (We need to remember here that the term "aristocracy" refers in its roots to a group of "the best" and does not have to mean only "a few.")

One hears the calls for new leadership, and a new vision of leadership, in virtually every community. Those calls seem to be pleas as much for a renewal of the full engagement of many citizens in civic life as for the emergence of a few special problem solvers. Clearly, America's colleges and universities can play a very powerful role in teaching their students about the traditions of civic responsibility

that have shaped our democratic culture; about the ways those responsibilities will fall upon them, if they wish to sustain and continue to be part of such a culture; and about how to participate constructively in the life and dialogue of democratic society. If our institutions of higher education abandon this historic role, the consequences may be very serious.

PUBLIC EXPECTATIONS

One of the most immediate consequences for institutions of higher education, if they abandon the work of civic education, is likely to be some further measure of public alienation and the loss of public support. Most of these institutions, after all, are either public or tax-exempt, nonprofit organizations; they are afforded their privileged status on the assumption that they contribute to "the common good." Obviously, higher education contributes to the common good in many ways; preparing students explicitly for the responsibilities of citizenship is only one of these. Still, when colleges and universities appear to be failing in this regard, the public reaction is likely to be negative and significant.

There is considerable evidence that negative public reaction has occurred—or is occurring—on several

Colleges and universities
have an obligation to examine
the ways they contribute
to the betterment of society

---

fronts, for a number of reasons. Clearly, the lack of attention to citizenship education is neither the first nor the only reason. Concerns that collegiate education does not adequately prepare students to be competitive in the marketplace and questions about the costs and value of such an education probably are the most significant. Yet one sees signs of public disillusionment and dissatisfaction when college education does not seem to have salutory effects on peoples' character or sense of public responsibility.

This disillusionment has been evident in the critical view of college students and recent graduates reflected in public discussions and in the popular media. In the early 1980s, this group of young people frequently was characterized as self-centered and materialistic, generally unconcerned about community and public life. While the blame for this occasionally is assigned to their upbringing more generally, one also frequently senses the implicit expectation that their education should have had a more edifying effect on their character. This implicit expectation becomes more evident when commentators make a special point of noting that public figures involved in scandal behave reprehensively despite having had "the best education money could buy."

Another sign of this public concern appears in literature and public discussions observing that while the overall level of education in this country has been rising, a number of key indicators—such as voting rates and Americans' involvement in civic associations, for example—show participation in civic life decreasing.

Clearly the erosion of civic spirit cannot be blamed primarily on inadequacies in higher education. Still, it is fair for members of the public to wonder whether colleges and universities are falling short in this area.

Public concerns about the failures of colleges in this respect are not exactly new. In her recent work, Morse quotes from Alexander Flexner's report in 1908 and a Carnegie Commission report in 1973 echoing criticisms of higher education on these points.[13]

Like all other major institutions in our society, colleges and universities have an obligation to examine the ways they contribute to the betterment of society. (Some have argued—we think convincingly—that philanthropic, cultural, and educational institutions have special obligations in this regard.) Colleges and universities must ask themselves if they are not failing in an important part of their mission if their graduates enter society without a heightened sense of responsibility for contributing to the public good, getting involved in the important issues and debates of civic life, and making an effort to be constructive participants in solving their communities' problems. Furthermore, institutions of higher education should be mindful that these issues have special import for their own future.

No one has more at stake in sustaining a society in which true intellectual freedom is possible than colleges and universities. There are frequent and obvious signs of the erosion of the civic and civil culture which up to now has made it possible to establish and sustain that intellectual freedom. The maintenance of such a culture depends on educating a citizenry that both wants and is capable of sustaining a genuinely open, democratic society: one where different ideas and values are not merely tolerated but actually valued and brought into constructive dialogue around issues of societal concern—what one scholar calls "a community of difference."[14] Insofar as our colleges and universities fail to give conscious and careful attention to educating students about the value, meaning, and manner of participating in and sustaining such a culture, they are abandoning that educational work which may be most necessary to ensure their own future.

CIVIC EDUCATION
AND LIBERAL EDUCATION

Inevitably, one of the first responses to a call for attention to one more theme or subject in the curriculum will be the cry that there is no room or time. Admittedly, the typical undergraduate curriculum has become an overloaded smorgasbord with a myriad of specialty items and, it sometimes seems, no main courses or organizing principles. So it is all the more important to point out that attending to civic education does not have to mean the displacement of other courses or important objectives from undergraduate programs.

Educating students for citizenship need not detract from the energy we devote to educating them for critical thinking, disciplinary competence, or other more narrow intellectual objectives. Indeed, in many cases these efforts can reinforce each other. To argue otherwise is to imply that the development (or lack of development) of personal intellectual capabilities has nothing to do with the ability to participate in public dialogue and activity relating to the life and needs of our communities. It is also to suggest that the attitudes and values that seem to undergird citizenship in a democratic culture—respect for others, empathy, integrity—are unimportant

A liberal education ought to develop in the student the capacity for understanding and sound judgment

in intellectual and academic pursuits. These are not, we suspect, assumptions any serious educator is likely to admit.

In fact, attending to civic education can be largely taken care of simply by doing what a liberal education at its best is supposed to do in the first place. To make sense of this claim, we first must take a step back and consider how we define the purposes of liberal education.

As we indicated in the last chapter, there are a number of ways to define the purposes of liberal education. The tradition of liberal education contains within it different, sometimes dissonant, strains. Nevertheless, all of us involved with or concerned about the work of liberal education can and should articulate our own answers to the question, "What are the purposes and desired outcomes of this educational enterprise?"

Our answers provide an overarching framework for what we do, without which the education we work to provide may become fragmented, incoherent, or internally conflicted. We need to have some notion of what we expect our students to derive from the educational experience we facilitate—and how we expect them to be changed by it—if that experience is to have any sense of coherence and direction for the students.

Many of us may be inclined to state the goals of a liberal education in terms of the capacities we hope such an education builds in our students. In the classical ideal, it might be the capacity to live "the good life" (as Plato or Aristotle would understand it); in more modern terms, it might be the capacity for lifelong learning, for continued intellectual and personal growth.

We suggest that one useful way to state the ultimate goal of a liberal education is to say it ought to develop in the student the capacity for understanding and sound judgment.

In the "information age" the most important function of education—at least higher education—no longer is one of supplying knowledge or information. Rather, it is helping students learn how to distinguish good or useful information from poor or useless information. Many of us now have more facts and knowledge presented to us—or available at our fingertips—than we know what to do with. The questions we struggle with most often are: "How can I tell if this is true? Even if it is true, how does it apply to the situation I am confronting here and now? How are the ways I might use this information helpful or less helpful, appropriate or inappropriate, even moral or immoral?"

A focus on educating students

with the intention of developing the capacity for understanding and sound judgment is at the heart of all the proposed goals of liberal education described above.

Certainly, one's ability to attain the classical ideal of the good life is dependent on one's capacity for judgment. This ideal assumes, after all, that what one seeks in such a life is "the best" and "the beautiful." Moreover, to live the good life in this sense does not mean that one merely seeks to possess objects that are marked by these qualities but, even more importantly, that one embodies these virtues—moral and aesthetic excellence—in the way one lives, both in one's personal relationships and in one's participation in the public realm.[15]

Yet how can anyone do this if he or she lacks the ability to distinguish between what is good, useful, or beautiful and what is not? Such distinctions, moreover, must be made with a sensitivity to context, for what is good or useful in one situation may not be so in another. So the capacity for understanding and judgment, the ability to make sense of information and see its relevance and value (or lack thereof) in the various situations in which one finds oneself, is central to living "the good life."

Similarly, the capacity for lifelong learning also is dependent on developing a capacity for understanding and judgment. In the 1960s, "counterculture" musician Frank Zappa told his audience on one album, "If you had any guts, you'd go to the library and educate yourself." Although intended as a challenge to "the establishment's" educational system, this notion ironically captures the essence of one way of describing the goals of a liberal education. Its intention is to make people capable of going to the library and educating (or continuing to educate) themselves.

The question is: When people encounter the mass of books and other materials they find in the library, on what basis are they to choose which to read? And assuming they choose to read a variety of materials—which are likely to contain competing ideas and perspectives—on any particular topic, how are they to decide what weight to give to those various ideas and perspectives? And assuming they know how to evaluate the relative merit of different theories and concepts, how are they to know how those theories and concepts can or should be applied to the problem or question they came to explore? At every step, a capacity for understanding and sound judgment is required in this process of lifelong learning, especially if it is learning that is to give birth to action.

So, finally, no matter how we choose to formulate the larger goals of liberal education, ultimately they involve developing in students capacities for judgment: for assessing the merit of claims to truth; for evaluating the validity and significance of evidence and argument; and lastly, but certainly not least importantly, for being able to see the salience and meaning of what is learned in the context of whatever larger issue one is exploring or whatever problem one is solving.

Given this formulation of the purposes of liberal education, the question of how to include a focus on civic education is far less problematic than might first be thought. If this definition of purposes is valid, preparing students for citizenship means developing at least two capacities which also should be central outcomes of liberal education anyway. They are:

☐ *The capacity for analytic and synthetic—or integrative—thinking.* It often is crucial—but almost never enough—to be able to break a problem into its constituent parts and examine each in itself in an effort to solve it. There are many places in most arts and sciences curricula where students are taught this first set of skills. Yet it also is crucial, especially when dealing with the problems of society, to see the interrelations among different social is-

sues and dynamics. Absent that ability, we often see our society creating new problems in the effort to solve old ones or find that proposed solutions are worse than the original problems because we did not see how other reinforcing or interfering dynamics were involved in the original circumstances.

As a recent AAC report on liberal education states, students must be "nurtured and supported as they develop the capabilities they need to enter, negotiate, and make connections across communities of discourse both within and without the academy."[16] They never will be creative scholars, or constructive citizens, if they lack these capabilities.

☐ *The capacity simultaneously to be personally engaged and, when needed, stand at a distance that allows objectivity on a subject or issue under study.* This echoes the need for "critical compassion" cited earlier. Simply put, this is the ability to care about something—passionately even—and think rationally about it at the same time.

Again, there are many places in most undergraduate programs where students are taught to "hold themselves apart" from the things they are studying so that they might be objective. Much of what we teach—and the ways we teach—tells students that objectivity (meaning "detachment") is to be more highly

valued than passion in the intellectual life. Yet we know that most of
the great breakthroughs in science
and the greatest contributions to
the arts and humanities were made
by persons who had great passions
for—or a profound emotional stake
in—what they were working on.

We ought to be concerned if the
educational system we have created
dampens students' love for the phenomena they study and lessens
their concern for the potential effects of their knowledge on the
world at the same time it enhances
their intellectual capacities. This is
the stuff of which horror stories
about runaway technology and mad
scientists are made. At a much less
dramatic level, this is what is occurring when an English professor—
interviewed as part of another AAC
project—worries that while his students are "learning to analyze literature they seem also to be losing the
love of literature that brought them
to study English in the first place."

In the public life of our society we
see disastrous results of policy recommendations by "objective" experts who propose solutions without
any first-hand, experiential knowledge of the circumstances and without empathy for those in those
circumstances. We must work at developing in students the capacity to
be both reasonable and passionate
about the things they encounter

and study. Again, AAC's report
notes, "While it is important for
students to develop a detached critical perspective on subject matter, it
is equally important for them to
care about subject matter and see
its implications for their own
lives."[17]

If we are committed to providing
students a truly liberal education,
we will try to nurture and enhance
these capacities as primary outcomes of their educational experience. If we did this, we would be
doing two of the three most important things we need to do to educate students for citizenship in any
case. (The third has to do with
helping them learn how to move
back and forth between knowing
and doing, about which we will
have more to say later.)

One crucial caution is in order
here. To say that educating students
for citizenship requires that we give
them a solid, meaningful, liberal education is not to say business as
usual in our colleges and universities will fulfill the need for civic
education. A liberal education of
the sort encompassed in this description of its purposes and outcomes is too rarely seen today.
Rather, we contend here that if we
were to pay careful attention and
give real energy to better preparing
our students to be citizens, we
would find we were improving the

quality of undergraduate education as a whole.

Thus, to return whence we began, our claim is that we do not need to displace other elements of a good undergraduate education to provide civic education. We need instead to consider what and how we teach so that we might better meet all the essential goals encompassed in a fuller vision of the purposes of a true liberal education. Such an education helps people develop substantial capacities for understanding and sound judgment and nurtures their commitment to exercising those capacities for the public good of the communities of which they are a part.

TEACHING ABOUT PHILANTHROPY AND VOLUNTARISM

THINKING INTEGRATIVELY
AND ANALYTICALLY

COMBINING KNOWING AND DOING

THINKING, DOING, AND LEARNING

With so many new subjects trying to stake a claim in the undergraduate curriculum—international studies, multicultural studies, ethnic studies, to name a few—why should teaching about philanthropy and voluntarism be given consideration? Even if the development of understanding and sound judgment, or practical wisdom, is accepted as the ultimate goal of a good undergraduate education, are there not many things we could teach as a way of achieving this end?

No doubt there are other disciplines, subjects, and ideas we can teach to develop practical wisdom. Moreover, it certainly is true that how we teach—the ways we interact with our students, the ways we encourage them to interact with one another, and the ways we ask them to treat the subject matter under study—does more to affect and nurture their capacity for sound judgment and participation in public life than the choice of subject matter itself.

Still, some subjects lend themselves particularly well to focusing on the capacities outlined in the last chapter that should be essential outcomes of liberal education, capacities which also are crucial to civic education. The history and social practice of philanthropy, defined in its broadest terms as "voluntary action for the public good," is such a subject.[18]

THINKING INTEGRATIVELY
AND ANALYTICALLY

The argument has been made compellingly elsewhere that the current emphasis in higher education on the development of analytical reasoning abilities, absent a balancing emphasis on integrative reasoning, is problematic.[19] We have cited the call in a recent report to help students develop the ability to make connections across different fields and between the subjects they study in classrooms and libraries and their experience of the world. The failure of higher education to develop this capacity in students contributes to serious problems for our society.

All too frequently we see evidence of the problems created for our society by specialists who seem capable of making choices only in terms of one or another very narrow way of viewing the world. The sad fact, however, is that these same specialists also often are described as "well educated," frequently having at least their undergraduate degrees in the liberal arts or sciences from prestigious institutions. If they were the recipients of a liberal education—one that should have broadened their horizons and helped them learn to appreciate and understand the complexities and ambiguities of intellectual work—how did their vision come to be so constricted?

The way undergraduate education in the arts and sciences (as well as the professions) is structured, we should not be surprised at such narrowness of perspective and inability to see things in a larger context. In most college classrooms, we see few efforts to help students learn to perceive and comprehend the world integratively: to see how the character and meaning of what they study may be shaped or changed by the larger context in which they exist and their relationships with other elements of that context.

One recent survey found that in completing assignments or examinations, most students in the arts and sciences seldom need to draw upon any knowledge or skills they might have gained in courses outside their own major. In fact, most students say that they usually are not even asked to draw upon knowledge or skills from other courses in the major.[20] In short, in most programs there is no expectation that students will build upon and integrate different sources and kinds of learning.

This not to say that analytic skills—knowing how to take things apart to examine the pieces, or breaking problems down into managable units which can be solved on the way to solving a larger problem—are unimportant. These are essential skills in life as well as the academy, and they are skills we try to teach in many ways and in many places in the curriculum. It is no less essential, however, to be able to see that divisions of the world made in the academy often are arbitrary and often distort our perceptions of reality.

Seeing how things relate, how they are shaped by one another as well as what they may be in and of themselves: these are capacities we cannot do without if we are to function constructively in the world. Yet these are capacities, as we have noted, that we teach much less often and less well.

Teaching about philanthropy and voluntarism can provide special opportunities for helping students learn how to think both analytically and integratively. Some examples from courses developed through AAC's Program on Studying Philanthropy illustrate the possibilities.

☐ An economics class examined the history of philanthropy in America and the social implications of philanthropy as an economic practice. Students in this class learned to analyze specific economic and historical phenomena while considering those phenomena as parts of a larger social environment and cultural history. These capacities were demonstrated in students' reaction to a prominent news story of the time about three whales trapped in arctic ice. In an impromptu discussion, students talked about the possibility of doing a limited cost/benefit analysis for staging a rescue; they also considered whether

the costs of rescuing three whales could be justified in relation to other worthy environmental work. Finally, they offered some remarkable insights about why people may be so ready to contribute to such an effort; they noted the irony that people in this society seemed to be more interested in saving three whales than in helping thousands of homeless people.

☐ In another course developed through the program, students who were mostly business majors read literature about individualism and philanthropy in American life. The course required students to explore the kinds of basic cultural values that undergird the existence of societal and organizational structures in America. These students soon were able to ask critical philosophical questions about the formative assumptions of management practices and simultaneously to raise significant practical and analytical concerns about the real and variable impact of those systems and organizations our society has adopted or created for "doing good."

☐ Yet another course included readings about international relations and the work of private, voluntary organizations in development work; at the same time, students explored the economic impact of that kind of work and the ways it may affect local cultures for good or for ill. This course engaged students in examining efforts to improve the international order in human, anthropological, and economic as well as political terms; it also helped them think about how similar kinds of political structures may work very differently in different cultural contexts.

In all these cases—and others—the study of philanthropy appeared to play a significant and effective role in helping students develop the ability to juxtapose specific issues and larger questions in a meaningful way and in facilitating their capacities to see situations through more than one disciplinary perspective.

The study of philanthropic practice may be approached in many different ways. It may be seen as a religious, economic, political, sociological, historical, or philosophical phenomenon—or some combination thereof—and the study of it can begin in any of those disciplines (or others). Because it finally touches facets of all those disciplines, however, the study of philanthropy must involve concepts and perspectives from many disciplines to be successful. If it is intelligently structured, it invites students to develop an interdisciplinary perspective, and it helps them learn how to use the analytical tools and perspectives they acquire in the academy to reflect on "real life" problems and issues. These aspects of philanthropic studies also seem to be key reasons for the appeal to stu-

dents of the courses developed under the AAC/AAFRC program.[21]

How unusual it is—at least on some campuses—that students' work results in their developing such a perspective was underscored by some of their own comments.[22] When asked at the end of one of these courses about how it related to the rest of her academic work, one student responded—with apparent surprise that such a possibility should even be considered—"It was really neat to find that things you learned in one course made sense in some other." In another course which included a significant field study component, a student commented on how refreshing and helpful that experience was: "By this point you're getting tired of one course after another in your field. This course...began preparing us to think about how we are going to deal with questions and issues in the real world."

The importance for the future of our democratic society of developing these capacities for integrative as well as analytic thinking in more of our students should be obvious. How often now do we find that meaningful action on social issues is stalled by people's tendency to debate those issues only in narrowly conceived, parochial, and often ill-informed terms? We cannot long sustain a free and open society in which this continues to be the case.

COMBINING KNOWING
AND CARING

One student interviewed after his participation in a course on "Philanthropy and Community" offered some extraordinarily honest and insightful comments about himself and how this course changed him. When asked why he took this course, he replied:

> My friends all think I am an "uncaring capitalist," and they challenged me to take this course. I think they were sure I would drop out...but it's turned out to be a really good experience. My volunteer experience has really changed the way I look at things. I guess it is making me more caring. It wasn't that I didn't care before, I think; it's more that I wasn't close enough to really understand the problem.

This student's comments indicate that the course was an experience that evoked personal engagement and commitment at the same time it demanded critical thought and reflection. This student's observations about his experience speak with a special eloquence about the need for there to be both knowing and caring in truly meaningful learning.

The professor in this sociology course could have lectured about the concepts of class stratification, dependency and empowerment, or paradigms for social service delivery; many

of the students would have grasped those concepts. One wonders, however, how many of them would have retained that knowledge, and for how long, and how many of them would have come to see how those concepts could be useful in understanding the world as they experience it. In focusing on philanthropy and community—and engaging students in first-hand experience as well as reading and reflection—this course showed students ways to think about things they cared about; it also encouraged them to care about the things these concepts represent and serve to explore.

Rare is the college professor—at least outside of professional schools—who has not at some point had the experience of having just completed a careful, perhaps eloquent presentation of some central concept or insight from her discipline, only to find that the students' first question is, "So, why is this important?" Most faculty members teach in the particular fields they do because they love the subject matter, ideas, or issues those fields encompass. For many students taking their classes, however, this is not the case; while the teacher may be able to convey his or her own enthusiasm, getting students fully engaged in the learning process requires giving them some reason to care about the subject at hand.

There obviously are many possible answers to the question, "Why is this important?" or "Why does this material matter?" It will matter to most students insofar as they are going to get graded on their knowledge of it, but that clearly evokes only a shallow and short-term interest. We also can expect that the more practical—or more mercenary—students will care about the things that translate into marketable skills and knowledge. Finally, though, if we believe that what we teach is important—if we really want students to appreciate as well as know the material and concepts—we must help them see how it is significant in terms of the personal and sociopolitical concerns and questions that matter in their lives.

This happens much less often than one might think—certainly less than we would hope. In only three of twelve arts and sciences majors could a majority of students in a recent survey say that "in the courses they took ...materials and assignments usually connected to personally significant questions." Worse yet, in more than half these programs less than a third of the students said this "usually" occurred.[23]

AAC's 1985 report *Integrity in the College Curriculum*—a report that was not seen as particularly radical, we might add—lamented the failure of teaching faculties to take up "opportunities...[to] bring students into humanistic relationships with their subjects, into the arena of values and

choice and judgment."[24] It is crucial for faculty members to take advantage of and create more such opportunities if they want to involve students more deeply in a learning process that might result in the development of well-honed personal capacities for understanding and sound judgment.

In addition to the importance of linking knowing and caring for the purpose of fully engaging students in the learning process, we also should consider what messages we are sending when we suggest that it is possible—even desirable—to acquire and act on knowledge about things one does not care about. Parker Palmer notes:

Knowledge contains its own morality, that it begins not in a neutrality but in a place of passion within the human soul. Depending on the nature of that passion, our knowledge will follow certain courses and head towards certain ends.... If we are worried about the path on which our knowledge flies and about its ultimate destination, we had better go back to its launching pad and deal with the passions that fuel and guide its course.[25]

When we convey the impression to students that it does not really matter—in Palmer's analogy—where knowledge comes from or where it goes, we are preparing them to be the worst kinds of citizens, professionals, and persons. The potential effects of what one knows, how one knows it, and what may be done with that knowledge may have profound consequences in many of the situations people face from day to day, not only for themselves but for others. To care about what we know, and to think about what we care about, means wrestling with these implications. As Elizabeth Minnich has put it:

Insofar as we give students theoretical knowledge and do not give them the opportunity to work on when and how and whether that knowledge illuminates or obscures the particularities that make up the real world, we prepare them either to be ineffective [as participants in public life], or to be tyrants who apply theory without regard for situations and individuals.... [26]

Only as students understand the power that knowledge may bring and the responsibility that comes with it are they likely really to care about what they learn and how they learn it. Only then are they likely to think seriously about how it is appropriate or inappropriate for them to use what they learn. Yet if the goal of a liberal education is the development of the capacity for sound judgment—or practical wisdom—this is what must happen. Surely this kind of understanding and caring is a prerequisite for constructive participation in public life.

This point is illustrated superbly by an exceptionally creative exercise in another of the courses developed through the AAC/AAFRC project. The institution at which the course was taught is in the heart of New York City; the students—many of them from minority groups—not only studied but lived and worked in the urban environment.

The class was a history course on the role of philanthropy and voluntary social welfare institutions in providing services to the needy, with a focus on the nineteenth and early twentieth centuries. Thus, one of the key concepts students needed to comprehend was the problem of defining "worthiness" among potential aid recipients.

Instead of merely lecturing and offering readings about the effects of social status, prejudice between ethnic and racial groups, and assumptions about the relationship between morality and wealth in American culture, the professor also had students keep journals of their encounters with people on the streets of Manhattan—individuals asking for money—as they went about their daily business. Students kept track of which individuals, among the many apparently "needy" people they encountered, to whom they chose to give (or not give), and the grounds on which they made those decisions. Were they making these choices on the basis of appear-

One powerful way to enrich
the quality of students' learning
is to link study, action, and reflection

ance, sobriety, ethnic or racial background, demeanor?

After several weeks, students shared
their journals in class. Then they
read pamphlets and other documents
from nineteenth-century service institutions, such as welfare hospitals and
homes for unwed mothers, describing
whom these institutions served and
why. Many of the students never had
encountered these kinds of primary
source materials previously. As they
did, they compared their own criteria
for "worthiness" to the criteria of
those nineteenth-century institutions.

Through their encounters with the
contemporary urban "laboratory" of
New York City and with documents
from one hundred years before their
own time, students more clearly understood how decisions about who
will be cared for are made, the nature
of the "facts" that are basis for such
judgments, and the social consequences of the ways such judgments
are formed. This was a particularly
poignant occasion of insight for these
students; many of them were first-
and second-generation immigrants,
and they saw how their parents and
grandparents—and they, too—would
have been considered "undeserving."

As a result, the students cared
about the subject matter of history—
at least of this history—and wanted to
think and learn more about it. Ultimately, the students thought more
about questions they already cared

about—questions such as, "In what
ways am I obligated to give something back to my own community, if
I am successful enough to 'make it'?"

When students leave classes thinking this hard and this well about the
things they care about, and caring
this much about the things they are
learning about, they truly are getting
a liberal education. Then they may
be able to continue to educate themselves, and they are going to have
some inclination and solid sense of
how to be constructive participants in
the civic life of the communities of
which they will be a part.

THINKING, DOING,
AND LEARNING

As we have seen, one powerful way
to enrich the quality of students'
learning is to link study, action, and
reflection.[27] This is a possibility that
often is not considered in liberal arts
courses, but there is no good reason
for this to be the case. As our examples indicate, elements of experiential
learning in liberal arts courses can be
extremely useful in teaching central
concepts in traditional disciplines.
They also, obviously, add elements to
such courses that require students to
be active rather than passive learners,
give them opportunities to learn how
to exercise judgment, and help them
learn how to integrate different types
of knowledge—that is, knowledge de-

riving from different types of sources.

Courses about philanthropy, broadly defined—including the donation of time and energy as well as money—can provide exceptional vehicles for integrating experiential learning components with traditional academic study in a discipline. They have the added value of building on a pre-existing experiential base because most students have experience as volunteers.[28] Moreover, experiential components were major factors in attracting students' interest and participation in the courses developed through AAC's Program on Studying Philanthropy.

Besides attracting students to these courses and generally enriching the quality of students' learning in them—no small benefit—the experiential learning elements reinforced the message that the connection between knowing and doing is socially and politically significant. This is important because in many ways the academy sends the opposite message to its students: that knowledge not only can but should be sought "for its own sake," and those seeking knowledge for such "pure" purposes need not concern themselves with its social significance.

The latter message may be necessary, in some measure, to counterbalance the pronounced tendency of the general public in recent years to ask that all pursuit of knowledge be justified in crassly pragmatic—that is,

purely economic—terms. And certainly a love of learning deriving simply from the pleasure one may experience in the process is a desirable outcome of a liberal education. Even that knowledge which is attained out of a love of learning, however, ultimately must have some effect on the life of the knower—and hence on the lives of others—to be significant.

Seeking knowledge for its own sake is neither the highest nor the purest of human endeavors; seeking it to help make the world a better place and improve the human condition—or to improve oneself—may be. Moreover, insofar as any knowledge we attain affects the way we see the world and behave in it, that knowledge has public consequences. Hence, it is vital that students understand that there is an inevitable link between what we know and what we do and that there are important ways that knowing and doing both can be sources of new learning.

Thus, it is important to show those we hope to immerse for several years in "the life of the mind" that we expect the knowledge and skills they attain to have consequences for the way they make decisions and act in the world. Similarly, it is important that we show students that we expect them to bring the things they learn from life to the reading and thinking they do. Courses that involve students simultaneously in studying, acting on, and reflecting on ideas, questions, and phenomena demonstrate this desire for the integration of different kinds of learning and knowing.

One course offered as a result of the AAC initiative focused on how voluntarism can be a force for positive change in the community or a force for the preservation of inequitable and repressive conditions. In addition to reading about the American traditions of voluntarism and civic participation and the processes and structures through which communities organize themselves, students were required to have an extensive time involvement in some voluntary service program.

One student chose to work in homes for the aged as a recreational aide. During the second week of his placement the staff in all the nursing homes in the city went on strike, in part to protest their own low wages but also to protest the conditions of patient care. The student was faced with the dilemma of choosing between providing a valuable—though not vital—service to those he wanted to help and supporting the efforts of others who wanted to effect more basic changes to improve the lives of these same people.

By maintaining a dialogue with both sides of the dispute, as well as doing the course readings and reflecting on his experiences in light of those readings, this student had what

he described as "a life-changing experience." He remained committed to continuing in some sort of service work—though he now would be more conscious of the "political" implications of that work. He also began to understand how the knowledge he gained through study could inform his personal choices and how the knowledge he gained through experience was necessary to test the concepts and meaning of the facts he encountered in his studies. Ultimately, he realized how he could act on what he learned and learn from his own actions.[29]

While the inclusion of experiential elements is important to "make the theoretical real" to students and to "make things make sense," it also can help students understand how knowledge can be power and thereby empower them to begin—or continue—to act on what they know and value. If one of the key purposes of liberal education is to prepare students for responsible citizenship, this empowerment is a crucial outcome. As Richard Morrill has noted:

Democratic literacy is a literacy of *doing, not simply of knowing.* Knowledge is a necessary but not sufficient condition of democratic responsibility. The task of civic [and liberal] education is, then, especially difficult and ambitious for it involves the empowerment of persons as well as the cultivation of minds.[30]

It is vital that those who receive a college education feel empowered to act on their knowledge—and that they know how to move from knowing to acting and how to learn from acting. This is essential if they are to be constructive and creative contributors to the common good of their communities, whether this means participating in the formal political processes of society or merely doing something personally to address the problems of those communities. Again, because of the very nature of the subject, courses about philanthropy and voluntarism can be ready vehicles for the kind of empowerment described here.

The results of the survey of students who took the courses developed through the AAC/AAFRC project and our interviews with them show that they are, as a result, generally more inclined to get involved (or stay involved) in civic activities.[31] In the interviews especially, a number of these students talked about how they came away with a new belief that a single person acting thoughtfully and out of conviction could make a difference in the life of her or his community. One particularly articulate young women said, "You look at these problems, and they are so overwhelming, and you feel like nothing you can do will make a difference. But this course has helped me see how each person, doing what she can, does make a difference [and] may even be the beginning of a big change."

In all these ways, then, courses about philanthropy and voluntarism can provide exceptionally useful and powerful vehicles for developing those capacities which should be among the essential outcomes of a liberal education—capacities that also are crucial attributes of persons who are, or will be, constructive and responsible citizens, members of the enlarged and inclusive "aristocracy of talent and virtue" our society needs to develop.

CHAPTER FOUR

■

COURSES, DYNAMICS, STUDENTS, AND OUTCOMES

COMMON PURPOSES AND PEDAGOGIES

THE SHAPE OF SPECIFIC COURSES

ADDITIONAL COMMENTS

The stories and examples presented in the previous chapter are drawn from the courses developed through the AAC/AAFRC Program on Studying Philanthropy. After members of the board of the AAFRC Trust for Philanthropy approached AAC with the initial idea for this program, AAC's staff worked with them to shape and expand that idea in a number of ways. With the support of a sizable initial grant from the Trust, as well as the Trust's help in raising other funds, AAC was able to create a curriculum development program substantially larger than what AAFRC had originally envisioned; the program also incorporated a number of unusual

features, such as the inclusion of experiential learning components.

In 1986 AAC invited applications for grant support for the development of liberal arts courses about philanthropy, voluntarism, and the nonprofit sector. The request for proposals mandated that the courses be rooted in the fields of liberal arts; it also strongly urged, however, that course designs incorporate interdisciplinary perspectives and approaches in content and teaching and include elements of experiential learning. Courses were to be offered each year for three consecutive years on a trial basis. The grant funds could be used to pay for faculty time, outside speakers or resource people, course

The study of philanthropy
in a well-designed course
is inherently interdisciplinary

materials, library resources, or anything else that directly supported the offering of the course.

More than fifty proposals were received in the summer of 1986, of which nine were selected for funding.[32] These grant recipients were expected to begin offering their courses in the 1987–88 academic year. Another request for proposals was put out the next year, again eliciting more than fifty applications. At that point seven more were selected for funding; these recipients began offering their courses in 1988–89. Ultimately, fourteen institutions successfully mounted their courses for the three-year trials.[33]

One additional element of this program should be mentioned. At the inception of this effort, AAC recognized that those who would be designing and teaching courses like these had little help in the way of bibliographical resources. There was then no listing or compilation of books, articles, or other materials about philanthropy to which they might turn for guidance in considering readings for their course. Therefore, part of the program funds were devoted to the development of an annotated bibliography about philanthropy and voluntarism. This formidable task was undertaken by Daphne Layton, who was then on the AAC staff and was the original assistant director for this project. Her

bibliography, *Philanthropy and Voluntarism*, was published by the Foundation Center in 1987 and was the first resource of this type in the field. It has proved to be an extremely valuable document for researchers as well as teachers, and it clearly is an important contribution by this project to the field of philanthropic studies.

The courses that were developed under AAC's Program on Studying Philanthropy represent a wide range of academic interests and disciplines— from American literature to public policy, from philosophy to sociology. One even had an international focus. Each course took its own distinctive approach to engaging students in an examination of the phenomona of philanthropy or voluntarism in the life and history of American society.

COMMON PURPOSES AND PEDAGOGIES

Despite the diversity of faculty interests, institutional contexts, and approaches to teaching represented in this program, the courses that were developed exhibited a number of shared purposes and outcomes, as well as several common pedagogical strategies. In one way or another, virtually all of these courses did at least three things.

☐ First, they drew students into the study of subject matter that is both academically challenging and personally engaging. They required students to wrestle with issues that are intellectually substantial and complex and in which they can identify a personal stake—for example, the nature of citizens' obligations to contribute to the social welfare of others or the character of the relationships between those who are economically privileged and those who are not.

☐ Second, these courses required students to bring together in the study of a single subject the knowledge, analytical skills, and perspectives they had acquired in different disciplines. The study of philanthropy in a well-designed course is inherently interdisciplinary. Philanthropy is a practice that raises historical, philosophical, and religious questions, as well as economic, sociological, and political ones. One scholar has described the history of philanthropy as "the social history of the moral imagination."[34]

☐ Finally, these courses involved students in making the connections between knowing and doing. The courses gave them practice in reflecting on and learning from what they were doing—from efforts to apply what they were learning. In a real sense, these courses were not satisfied with students' acquiring merely theoretical knowledge but sought to help them develop practical wisdom.

As one would expect, there also were some pedagogical strategies that were commonly employed in many of the courses to engender these shared outcomes. The key approaches to teaching and learning—used in varying combinations—that seemed crucial to the notable success and popularity (with students) of these courses included:

☐ *Consciously interdisciplinary reflection*: Almost all the courses intentionally engaged students in examining the issues under study from more than one disciplinary perspective. This was done by the choice of readings, the use of guest speakers, team teaching, and the ways the instructors introduced and discussed issues and materials.

☐ *Experiential learning components*: Many of these courses required students to experience first-hand the kinds of issues, problems, and organizations they were studying. This took a number of forms, from "requiring the students to volunteer"—recognizing the inherent contradiction in that notion—with a philanthropic or voluntary organization to doing a field study of some aspect of such an organization.

☐ *Bringing the community into the classroom*: Where, for whatever reason, it was not feasible to involve the students in service learning or field studies, many of these courses made extensive use of guest speakers, field trips, and other approaches to creating first-hand encounters with the community and the issues under study by bringing people from the community into the classroom. In some cases these efforts were part of courses that also involved a more direct or intensive experiential learning component.

How these elements were incorporated into the courses, and their relative effectiveness, depended in many ways on the institutional context of the course. The kinds of students attending an institution, the kind of community in which an institution is located, and the characteristics of institutional structures and climate relating to teaching, learning, and service will have significant influence on whether the elements of course design listed above can work and how they should be used.

THE SHAPE
OF SPECIFIC COURSES

The courses in the AAC project, and the experiences of students in these courses, illuminate these matters in a variety of ways. We shall describe briefly most of the courses that were offered for the full three-year trial. (A few were so similar to each other that some of those descriptions would seem repetitive.)

It is important to note that the order in which these descriptions are presented does not represent any ranking or priority; it simply reflects the order in which the institutions were visited during the evaluation process. The chronological order is preserved here because some of the insights that these visits provided were cumulative.

REGIS COLLEGE

At Regis College outside of Boston, economics professor Mary Oates offers a course entitled "Perspectives on American Philanthropy." This upper-division offering in economic history examines the place and function of philanthropy in the American political economy since the nation's founding. It also highlights the roles women have played in society through their involvement in philanthropic and voluntary organizations.

In addition to examining the role of philanthropy in "helping people progress in their economic well-being to move toward integration into society" and the role of women in these efforts, the course addresses topics such as philanthropic responses to immigration, philanthropy and African Americans, and the relationship between private philanthropic efforts to improve social welfare and government efforts in this realm. Taking an interdisciplinary tack, the course requires students to explore the character, evolution, and significance of giving, examining "social and economic issues as well as cultural effects."[35]

Readings for the course are drawn from a wide range of primary source materials, as well as from Robert Bremner's history, *American Philanthropy*. At least six guest speakers—from foundations, service agencies, religious organizations, and the ranks of private donors—visit the class. In addition, students are required to visit and write a research paper about a Boston-area philanthropic agency; they also are urged to volunteer at such an agency to get a fuller picture of how these groups function in our society.

Further, students are required to do a research project on a topic of their choice relating to the issues raised in the course. Students present their work in a variety of ways. One group developed a very impressive photo essay on one of Boston's major homeless shelters; another student researched and analyzed the role of women in the development of the Audobon Society.

This course has been a remarkably powerful learning experience for the students involved. It has been consistently well enrolled, and it has received consistently high ratings from students. Students expressed great appreciation of the requirement to serve in and study voluntary and philanthropic organizations first-hand, as well as the ways those experiences were tied into classroom discussions and reading. They commented that these experiences "brought the ideas we learned to life" and "made us understand the real importance of what we had been talking about [in class]." Students also spoke highly of the interdisciplinary aspects of the course, remarking on how refreshing it was to "have a chance to bring different things [we had studied] together."[36]

It is clear that this course thrives at Regis not only because it is well conceived and well taught—though it is both. It also thrives because it fits well into Regis' sense of mission and organizational culture. There has been practical and moral support for this effort from all quarters of this small, Catholic, women's college. Virtually everyone on campus—professors from other departments, the librarian, the chaplain, and the president of the college—is aware of the course and what the students are doing in it. There is good communication between faculty members and different departments, making the interdisciplinary character of the course easy to implement. The course also builds on the college's commitment to service in the community, which is reflected in the support provided by the college chaplain's office and service programs for the outreach elements of the course.

"Perspectives on American Philanthropy" appears likely to have a long life in the Regis College curriculum because it develops the kinds of intellectual abilities and moral commitments in students that the Regis College's administration and faculty believe should be a result of a good liberal education in the Catholic tradition.

NORTHWESTERN UNIVERSITY

Northwestern University offers its course on "Philanthropy in America: Private Interests and the Public Good" as a "senior linkage seminar." Five or six such seminars are offered each term to provide a capstone experience for seniors that involves them in interdisciplinary examinations of "real world" problems. The existence of this series of seminar offerings provides a natural setting for this course, which is offered under the aegis of the American studies program.

"Philanthropy in America" focuses on the role of large foundations and their influences on public policy in our society, highlighting the question of whether they more often serve the public good or private interests in their grantmaking activities. Pursuing this question means engaging the students in first-hand, in-depth examinations of the reasons for and manners of foundation grantmaking. In the words of the instructor, it is important for the students to realize "philanthropy must be viewed in the context of politics, special interests, and even self-interest," as well as in terms of altruism and public service.[37]

The course begins with a brief historical examination of philanthropic philosophy and practice in America, then goes on to consider more closely its role in shaping public policy. Topics in the latter section include the professionalization of philanthropy, board versus staff roles in shaping foundations' priorities and programs, and issues of public accountability for private foundations' activities. A major requirement of the course is that each student develop an in-depth profile of a Chicago-area foundation. This involves students in field research, making direct contacts with those foundations to get information about the foundations' decision-making processes, priorities, and relationships with grantee organizations.

This has been an extraordinarily popular offering from its inception. (The seminars are limited to eighteen students, and this one has been so over-subscribed that Northwestern began offering a second section without grant support.) Part of the students' interest clearly derives from the course's focus on significant personal and social issues. One student observed that the attraction of this course was that it "looks at things we're really going to be dealing with next year and starts us thinking about how we're going to look at questions and issues in the real world." Several others echoed this sentiment.

In addition, the course seems eminently useful as a capstone experience, honing students' analytical and integrative capacities. During seminar discussions, students displayed considerable sophistication in exploring the issues from different disciplinary perspectives. In appreciation of the course, one student said, "What we're doing here makes you more critical—in a good way, in looking at the relationships between things and where you want to stand in them." Our observations confirm that the course is indeed having that effect.

This course—or a related one—seems likely to be offered with some frequency at Northwestern, partly because it offers such a useful topical focus for the "senior linkage seminars" and partly because student demand has been so high. In addition, several administrators said having the course in the curriculum reinforces an emphasis on service to the community and philanthropic activity that Northwestern wants to embrace.

SETON HALL UNIVERSITY

At Seton Hall University, a course called "American Philanthropy: Historical and Political Perspectives" is offered by the political science department in cooperation with the Center for Public Service; the course is cotaught by an historian and a political scientist. An upper-division seminar, it has enrolled twelve to fifteen students each time it has been offered.

The team-teaching arrangement is representative of the designer's intention that this course engage stu-

Perhaps there is no more obvious
intellectual home
for a course on philanthropy
than in the discipline of philosophy

---

dents in interdisciplinary study of the topic. Readings are drawn from Brian O'Connell's *America's Voluntary Spirit* and Alan Pifer's *Philanthropy in an Age of Transition*, as well as from periodicals and other books. The readings, discussions, and presentations in class are intended to involve students in an examination of the functions of the nonprofit sector in American society and introduce them to the historical and political background for pursuing that examination. That broad-based exploration is made more concrete through the use of case studies focusing particularly on health care and education as areas of philanthropic and nonprofit initiative.

The clear strength of this offering is in the solid introduction it provides to the overarching conceptual frameworks within which scholars have studied philanthropy and the nonprofit sector. Through team teaching, the use of cases, and careful selection of readings, this course also succeeds in getting students to work in truly interdisciplinary modes; students look at the conceptualization and proposed solutions of social problems by philanthropists and civic activists in both historical and sociopolitical terms. Students' responses to the course have been very positive, and their learning appears to have been substantial.

This course includes less fieldwork and fewer guest speakers than many other courses in the program, however, and the effects are evident in students' comments. Working on the cases, for instance, students seem less able to see how the contingencies of particular contexts would affect efforts to apply theoretical solutions to specific problems.

The decision not to include more of an experiential component seemed to be, in large part, a function of institutional context. Since the course is situated in an institution where conventional views of what constitutes "acceptable content and pedagogy" are dominant, its legitimacy might have been called into question if there had been significant emphasis on experiential learning. In addition, many students are commuters, presenting a host of problems with requiring and arranging fieldwork.

Nevertheless, one of the interesting findings in our evaluation of this course was the degree to which the professors have been able to involve students with the material in ways that raise, and allow students to pursue, personally significant issues. In addition to solid conceptual learning, the class has evoked a good bit of thoughtful, personal reflection on the part of students—something they saw as a real strength of the experience. One commented, "I think this class has helped me structure my own values—to think again about who gives money and why, and what I may want to do with my own money." Another said, "[The class] did change the way I look at things. Now I think about how giving time may be more important than giving money. Lots of people like me don't have much money, but they can make a real difference by giving their time to work on things they care about."

Ironically, perhaps, this interdisciplinary offering is likely to continue in the Seton Hall curriculum because its roots are firmly set in a traditional department. Furthermore, as the university is in a time of transition—reexamining its own mission and considering ways it can better serve the local community—the administration is quite pleased to have elements in the curriculum that focus on public service. This gives some additional legitimacy and emphasis to issues of community service that the university wants to stress. Clearly the course would be stronger if there were more community service activity involving students—on which it could build an experiential component—but it may turn out that the presence of the course can help generate some of that activity.

CHAPMAN COLLEGE

At Chapman College, the course on philanthropy is offered under the auspices of the humanities rather than the social sciences. "A Life of Service" is a philosophy course taught by Mike W. Martin that explores the proposition "that voluntary service and giving are central to the self-fulfillment of morally concerned individuals." Special attention is given to an examination of "the moral aspects of caring, helping, and volunteering; and also to virtues like benevolence, generosity, and gratitude."[38]

Perhaps there is no more obvious intellectual home for a course on philanthropy than in the discipline of philosophy. Insofar as philanthropy is almost always—at least in principle—an effort to do good, it is, in essence, an exercise in applied ethics. This course treats it as such, incorporating interdisciplinary perspectives as it challenges students to consider the practical circumstances—political, historical, economic, and religious—that create the context for making and evaluating such efforts to do good.

This is an exceptional course in several respects. Offered in an "Interterm"—the class meets for three hours a day, four days a week, for four weeks—it is a brief but very intensive exploration of the material. The short time span makes it very difficult to involve students in voluntary service or field research, but the professor attempts to make connections to the community and "real life" in a number of ways.

First, there are a number of biographical readings, which help place the theoretical consideration of virtues and moral values into concrete contexts with which students can identify. Second, a number of guest speakers are brought to the class to talk about their personal experiences in trying to live "a life of service." (There also is considerable additional informal time for students to visit with these people and probe the questions and issues their class presentations raise.)

The course requirements include keeping a journal in which students are expected to reflect on and integrate the readings, class discussions, and their own experiences and reactions to them. In addition, a portion of the journal is devoted to developing a case study of one American philanthropist (living or dead), relating the themes and questions explored in class to the life of that individual. This involves addi-

tional research by the student and becomes a kind of informal, reflective research paper.

The reading load for this course is heavy, part of the intensive nature of the experience. Readings include pieces from a wide range of philosophers, from Aristotle to Kant to John Stuart Mill, as well as materials from philanthropists and social scientists. Martin notes that he "tries to offer a philosophical piece every day in combination with the case studies of philanthropists."

Another way this course is distinctive from other offerings developed in AAC's project is that it does not explicitly raise public policy issues or deal much with institutional philanthropy. Rather, the key issues here are individual ethics, obligations, and commitments and how these are exemplified in individuals' lives. In taking this approach, Martin virtually forces his students to engage with the hard philosophical questions raised about the practice of philanthropy in a personal as well as an intellectual mode.

The obvious risk in such a course is that it easily could become a vehicle for preaching a particular moral perspective or set of values. To avoid this, Martin relies heavily on the Socratic method for the presentation and exploration of materials. The philosophical treatises, biographies, and case studies largely are left to speak for themselves (with appropriate background information and clarification provided); students are expected to raise questions for discussion from the texts, each other, and the lectures.

The effectiveness of this course and its approach to teaching philosophy as well as philanthropy was apparent in conversations with students. Not only were they extremely thoughtful about the questions of moral values, virtues, responsibilities to others, and motives for giving and service raised in the course, they also were very articulate about the importance of these issues in their own lives. One student commented, "Dr. Martin doesn't preach voluntarism. But what the course preaches is, 'You should make a choice for yourself about what you believe [about caring for and serving others], and whether or not you're going to be involved.'"

The value of a course like this for a college like Chapman is clear, and it was affirmed by the president of the college in our conversation with him. Chapman is a small, liberal arts college with religious roots. Its motto is "A Life of Service"—hence the title of the course. The president described the mission of the college in terms of "providing a liberal education of enduring quality in a value-centered environment." He acknowledged that the attention

to building a value-centered environment had been less evident than should have been the case in recent years, but he saw the college's commitment to developing this course as one effort (along with a number of others) to improve that.

One need only look closely at this course offering at Chapman College, and its effects on the students who take it, to dispel any doubts about whether the study of philanthropy belongs in an undergraduate liberal arts curriculum.

ILLINOIS STATE UNIVERSITY

At Illinois State University, political scientist Robert Hunt developed the only course in the AAC/AAFRC program with an international theme. "Voluntary Organizations and Global Development" focuses on "ways international voluntary or philanthropic activity has changed over time—from relief to development to what...is now a networking or catalyst role."[39] Using people with experience in international development and professors from other departments as guest speakers, Hunt integrates the academic exploration of international politics and economics in development work, the roles of voluntary organizations in that work, and the history and functions of voluntary organizations in American culture.

Readings include a number of books and articles on international development work, especially the roles of nongovernmental organizations in that work. Students also read works on the history and development of voluntary associations and philanthropic organizations in the United States. Requirements of students in the course include writing a series of brief essays in response to questions on key issues discussed in the class, preparing reviews of a number of significant articles on voluntarism, and producing a final policy paper on the role of voluntary organizations in international development work.

Students also are expected to get involved with a local voluntary service organization. The experiential component is intended to help them gain some first-hand experience with the issues and dilemmas of operating a voluntary agency which are salient regardless of the context within which the agency works—for example, raising funds or dealing with volunteers, the board, the constituency to be served, and staff. Setting up students' placements in local voluntary agencies is facili-

tated by the presence of a strong student community service network (coordinated by the campus ministries program) at the university.

The importance of the experiential component cannot be overstated. With its focus on agencies that do all their work overseas and on the dynamics and variables of working in foreign cultures and political systems, it would have been easy for this course to lose students' interest by becoming entirely theoretical. Virtually all the students we talked with spoke of the importance of the experiential element in making the concepts discussed real. One commented, "The experience of volunteering is very important, because it gives us a practical base." Students also noted how much they valued the professor's ability to "bring home the relevance of the questions being discussed. He was good at getting people to think about how voluntarism relates to them."

This course seems to have a bright future because it fits well in the interests of the department within which it is offered. Interestingly, though, its interdisciplinary character may make it most valuable to the university at large. In an institutional context where there is very little done across departmental lines, this course suggests some of the value and excitement of interdisciplinary work for faculty members as well as students. One administrator said, "This program has additional value for us as a first step in broadening people's perspectives and encouraging faculty members to consider new possibilities for interdisciplinary work."

CUNY- BERNARD BARUCH COLLEGE

Baruch College of the City University of New York has an arrangement to offer a small number of special upper-division seminars each term that have a limited enrollment (fifteen students maximum). These seminars usually are interdisciplinary in character and often are team taught. This seminar series became the home for the courses on philanthropy offered as part of the AAC program. (The specific topic and design changed each of the three years. In what follows we discuss the second offering, which was team taught by historian David Rosner, the original grant recipient, and sociologist Susan Chambre.)

"Voluntarism and the Problems of Dependency" was a seminar focusing on the development of social welfare institutions in the nineteenth and twentieth centuries.

(One exciting element of this course—students' compilation, analysis, and comparison of their own giving criteria—was described on pages 21–22). This course was remarkably powerful in engaging the students in thoughtful historical consideration of a number of the social systems and organizations that surrounded them and key institutions in their own community.

Readings were drawn from a large number of historical and contemporary books and periodicals about urban social problems and efforts to address them. One of the impressive elements of this course was the way it taught students to read and understand primary source materials. It also gave them practice in sifting through and considering the validity of different perspectives on social phenomena.

This development of the capacity to appreciate differing disciplinary and personal perspectives was encouraged further by the practice of team teaching in the seminar. Interviews with students indicated they first were puzzled but later found themselves instructed by observing the differences of opinion articulated by the two teachers in the seminar. Having the views of both Rosner and Chambre—sometimes in conflict—brought to bear upon the issues under discussion appeared to open the dialogue in the seminar and encour-

There are distinctive factors
in a large, urban university
that influence the success or failure
of a course about philanthropy

---

aged the students to define and offer their own perspectives.

There are a number of distinctive factors in a large, urban university like CUNY–Baruch that influence the success or failure of a course about philanthropy. Often there is no "campus community" which draws students together and from which they would go out into the community to do service. Many of these students already are rooted in the community, have full-time jobs in addition to being students, and appear on campus only for classes. The majority of them also are quite pragmatic in their reasons for pursuing higher education and in what they expect from their courses. Many come from economically disadvantaged backgrounds.

In this setting, the appeal of a course about philanthropy may be primarily for the opportunity it creates to learn and talk about the problems philanthropic activity addresses rather than for the opportunity to learn about philanthropy itself. Unlike some other more privileged and isolated campus settings— where one might assume the students will be able to handle complex intellectual challenges, but the difficulty is to make real the social problems to be studied—here the students were confronted every day with the problems of urban society; what they wanted was an opportunity to

study and reflect on those problems and potential solutions.

It is in the best tradition of liberal arts education to provide the occasions and the tools for individuals to engage with and reflect critically on questions and problems crucial for human existence. This course about philanthropy gave students a particularly useful structure and intellectual resources with which to think deeply and carefully about their own personal experiences with those pressing problems. All of the students we interviewed spoke of how powerful a learning experience this was. One summed it up by saying, "I'm learning lots of new stuff and seeing connections between things— like how this city really works, and how decisions get made, and why the things I see make me feel the way I do."

BABSON COLLEGE

Babson College is a small, private, business college near Boston. It has a strong liberal arts division and requires all its students—all of whom major in some business field—to take a substantial part of their coursework in the liberal arts. In particular, it has a strong American studies program, which became the home for a course on "Individualism and Philanthropy in American Life."

Offered as the "capstone seminar" for the American studies program, this course focused on the tensions between the values of community and conformity and the values of individualism in American life. Questions were raised about the ethical, political, and economic facets of the way our culture conceives of individual freedom and responsibility. These issues were explored through discussions of literature—*The Blithedale Romance* and *Up From Slavery*—as well as *Habits of the Heart* by Robert Bellah, et al., and Bremner's *American Philanthropy*. A number of films also were used.

Students also were required to do a field study of a Boston-area service agency, looking particularly at the relationships between that agency and the community in which it was located and the clientele it served. A number of students became involved in volunteering at those agencies, but the emphasis was on studying those agencies and their relationships to the surrounding community—and how well they serve that community. Students reported to the seminar on their research, where their findings were discussed.

One of the elements of this course

that stands out was its use of literature as the entree into the study of philanthropic practice and larger cultural issues. We observed the students' discussion of Booker T. Washington's autobiography and were impressed by the way in which this reading raised a number of issues central to the theme of this course and made them salient and accessible. Consideration of this book raised questions for students about the problems of dependency versus self-help and about the tensions between cultural autonomy and social control that the practice of philanthropy may create. Comparisons between this autobiography and the Horatio Alger stories brought out questions about how literary forms may be shaped by and reinforce certain cultural myths and values—like the traditional American emphasis on individualism and self-sufficiency.

Another notable aspect of this course was the way it engaged students' interest in moral and ethical issues. This is especially crucial and valuable in a context where so much of the students' education focuses on instrumental concerns, as is usually the case in professional programs. This is precisely the realm in which a good business education needs to be enriched by exposure to the questions and ideas which should be the focus of the liberal arts.

Here the practical as well as philosophical character of philanthropy as an area for study may be particularly useful in capturing a student's attention in the first place. One student explained why he decided to take the course by saying, "I figure I'm going to make a lot of money, and I thought I should learn something about what kinds of good things I can do with it." While it was not the purpose of this course to teach students "how to give," the course did give students practice in thinking about issues of moral conduct and social utility. In so doing, it gave that particular student a much better basis from which to make decisions about what to do with his expected resources.

The emphasis on moral and cultural issues, in fact, was a major drawing point for this course in this specialized environment. Many students said that they were drawn to the class because it provided an opportunity to explore a different perspective on money and society than they got in their business curriculum. They took the occasion to wrestle with these issues in personal as well as societal terms.

One student said the class "helped people to think about their future and their money; how much you really need to live on and how much is 'extra,' and what you can and should do with that." Another called it a particularly valuable course in

that "it made a lot of students uncomfortable, because it challenged the simple view of things they get in other classes and would like to maintain. Nowhere else around here are questions raised about corporate responsibility and obligations to the community."

In fact, there is considerable and increasing attention to ethics in Babson's curriculum. Still, the power of this course, at least in part, was a reflection of the different and more effective ways that the study of philanthropy, pursued through a variety of approaches—literature, film, field study—can engage students' intellects and imaginations to make the questions of ethical and societal issues more meaningful and more easily understood. In this way, liberal arts courses about philanthropy and voluntarism may prove even more valuable to students in business and other professional schools than to traditional liberal arts students.

TEMPLE UNIVERSITY

The course at Temple University was distinguished by its emphasis on fieldwork and service as the core of the students' experience, augmented by readings and reflection. The goals of this offering—entitled "Voluntarism and Community Organizing"—were to help students better understand the processes of community change and to examine the question of whether private voluntary and philanthropic activity is more often a force for changing the status quo or for preserving it.

Students in this course were required to spend ten hours a week in a local service agency and to keep a journal reflecting on their experiences in that work. In addition, they met once a week for a two-hour seminar session which provided opportunities for reflection on and discussion of their experiences and of assigned readings. The readings were drawn from a variety of works on the traditions of civic involvement and voluntary association, community organizing, and philanthropy and voluntarism. There also were a number of guest speakers from community organizations.

Ronnie Steinberg, the professor of sociology who designed this course, limited the types of nonprofit agencies for which the students could work; given the focus of the course, it was important that they be involved with an agency whose work was in direct service, advocacy, or community organization. Such placements involved students in the kinds

of situations that would raise the questions on which the course focused—questions about providing service versus working for change or about whether such agencies can work to meet immediate needs and strive to eliminate the causes of those needs at the same time. For example, Steinberg encouraged her students who were working in a shelter for the homeless to ask, "Given its goals and objectives, is it [working toward] achieving the elimination of homelessness or is it doing something more limited—namely [just] keeping people alive?"[40]

The impact of this course on the students involved was extraordinary. We have cited one student's story (see page 24); others had similar experiences. One said, "I don't mean to sound corny, but this course was a real turning point for me. I just see things differently now." Another observed, "I see this city and its people in new ways, and think a lot more about how what I can do will make a difference or not."

It is clear that the combination of the extensive—and intensive—field-work and reflection made this a powerful learning experience. In addition, many students said it was the experiential component that attracted them to the course.

Unfortunately, it also is clear that the sheer amount of fieldwork required was the course's biggest problem. This course was consistently under-enrolled, averaging only six students each term. The students we interviewed said that the friends to whom they had recommended the course had viewed as prohibitive the time required to do the fieldwork. Still, it seems possible that one could build a course on this model that did not require quite so much time in fieldwork and still achieve a similar effect. What was obvious was the power of this offering both in deepening students' comprehension of key issues and concepts in sociology and urban studies and in preparing them to be active, constructive members of their own communities.

UNIVERSITY OF SOUTHERN CALIFORNIA

At the University of Southern California, an economist and a sociologist co-teach the course on "The Nonprofit Sector and the Public Interest." Of the courses in AAC's project, this course probably is the most carefully conceived and analytic attempt to provide a comprehensive overview of philanthropic and voluntary organizations and of the independent sector's place in the American political economy. A mid-level course in the School of Public Administration, this offering also fulfills a general-education distribution requirement for undergraduates in "American Public Life."

The readings for the course include Bremner's history of philanthropy; *Free Spaces*, by Evans and Boyte; *The Nonprofit Sector: A Research Handbook*, edited by Walter Powell; and other pieces from a number of sources. The course includes a field study component; this requires students to develop a case study of a local nonprofit agency, examining its history, organization, and function in the local community and nonprofit sector. (It is suggested to students that they may want to volunteer for that organization to get an insider's perspective.)

As is suggested by the distribution requirement this course fulfills, one of the explicit focuses of the course is the role of voluntary associations and philanthropic initiative in civic or public life. The comprehensive nature of the syllabus, the team teaching, and the fieldwork involve students in looking at the nature of "the public interest"—or "the common good"—from different angles and disciplinary perspectives. Students get an introduction to ways of thinking about "the public interest" as defined by technical, professional, and academic criteria; they also explore questions raised by personal, ethical, and political experience about what constitutes "the public interest." In short, this is a course that specifically addresses the need for civic education and fosters the capacity to look at problems in an integrative manner that will allow creative and constructive participation in dialogue about public affairs.

Here again, students commented very favorably on the inclusion of the fieldwork element, noting the importance of this experience in making difficult concepts—and the complex relationships between public and private interest—more tangible and more readily understood. Students were carefully prepared for the field study experience, and the presentations to the class after the fieldwork created the occasion for broader sharing of the fruits of this experiential learning.

Interestingly, while this course is designed to serve a broad audience in the general-education program, its continuation may be assured by its special value to the School of Public Administration. The dean of the school told us this course "makes an important contribution to the range of offerings in public administration" because many public administration majors end up working in nonprofit organizations or sectors of the government that have to deal with those organizations frequently. In ad-

dition, "topics of central concern to public administration are raised and illuminated in the study of voluntary and nonprofit organizations."

TUFTS UNIVERSITY

"Philanthropy and Community" at Tufts University is an upper-division sociology course with ties to the American studies program. This course "explores the culture, history, social organization and political economy of philanthropy in the United States"; it focuses on questions such as, "Why and how do people give of their money and time? What can greater understanding of philanthropy and voluntary action tells us about our society and ourselves?"[41] Susan Ostrander, the course's designer, also is especially interested in looking at how philanthopic activity may be either a progressive or conservative force and what roles women have played in shaping the philanthropic tradition.

Requirements for the class include substantial reading, participation in a community project, and a series of short reaction papers to the readings, as well as active participation in the class discussions. On the reading list are *American Philanthropy*, *Habits of the Heart*, and *Free Spaces*, as well as a number of excerpts and articles from other sources.

The experiential component bears particular scrutiny here because of the way it was structured to serve several purposes. Students are expected to arrange their volunteer work so that they complete some specific project or task during their placement that makes a significant contribution to the work of the organization with which they are placed. This is intended to be an occasion for students to gather information about how a specific organization reflects—or does not reflect—the attributes and dynamics of philanthropic and voluntary initiative examined in the readings and in class. It also is intended to provide the stimulus for the students to reflect personally on how they feel about and relate to various ways of being involved in community action and service. Ultimately, though, it is supposed to be an experience that also will empower students—helping them understand something of their own possibilities and responsibilities for making a difference in public life around the matters they care about.

To interview the students in this course is to encounter a group of young people who have been through a powerful learning experience, one that bore great personal as well as intellectual significance for them. This course clearly encourages integrative as well as analytical thinking; it also invites students to make connections between what they care about and what they are learning about. We cited earlier the comments of one student who had been through this course and was transformed from an "uncaring capitalist." Another student commented that "this process has made me start thinking in ways I never thought before. I'm making all sorts of connections between my studies, my personal life, and what's going on in the world."

This course thrives at Tufts for a number of reasons. There is a strong service ethos on campus, with a great many students involved in community service and an academic center devoted to the study of nonprofit organizations. There also is substantial acceptance of interdisciplinary scholarship and courses. This creates a supportive climate for this offering. The reputation of the professor as a fine scholar and teacher also helps draw students and lends legitimacy to a course that otherwise might be viewed with skepticism.

Ostrander insists she should teach this course not so much because philanthropy, in and of itself, is deserving of study but, just as important, because it is a wonderful subject area for exploring and illuminating many of the central themes of her discipline—sociology. It obviously is an appropriate offering for an American studies program. Ultimately, however, it is well received and likely to continue at Tufts because, for a school that takes the commitment to liberal learning seriously, this course clearly serves the purposes of giving students a truly liberal education.

RANDOLPH-MACON WOMAN'S COLLEGE

Randolph-Macon Woman's College offers a course called "Public Service and the Common Good: Philanthropy and Volunteer Service in America." This course is co-taught through the religion department by professor Ivor Thomas and the president of Randolph-Macon Woman's College, Linda Koch Lorimer. Presented as an upper-division seminar, this course offers a general overview of the religious, social, and historical origins of the tradition of philanthropy and voluntary service in America and then moves on to more detailed study of specific areas of society—such as education and the arts—where philanthropic activity has been especially important.

Readings include *Habits of the Heart* and excerpts from *America's Voluntary Spirit*, as well as materials from other sources. Here too, students are expected to volunteer with a service organization to get firsthand experience with the topics under study, although in this case that experience was not necessarily a focus of classroom reflection and discussion.

To bring the community into the classroom, however, the instructors take a unique approach. Each time this class has been offered, three prominent women activists or volunteers have been invited to be part of the class on an ongoing basis. These women, who come from the local community with a wealth of experience in civic activism and voluntary service, bring a seasoned perspective to the class dialogue. They do the readings and participate in all the class sessions. (They are not asked to do papers or take tests, however, and they are not charged tuition.) In addition, other persons from philanthropic agencies are invited in connection with the class to speak in a public lecture series.

Given the institutional context, it is not surprising that a major theme of this course is the role of women in the philanthropic tradition. This is one vein in which this subject can be connected in a particularly powerful way with students' own interests and perspectives. In this regard, there is careful and critical examination of the societal as well as religious values and assumptions that undergird philanthropic and voluntary activity.

In an institution that expects to play a special role in educating women to be leaders in our society, a course like this has a significant part to play in providing the opportunity for those women to reflect on the privileges, obligations, and opportunities they have accepted or may be ready to accept in leadership roles in public life. Clearly this course serves that purpose well.

ADDITIONAL COMMENTS

The course descriptions above show how the key elements outlined at the beginning of this chapter have been employed in different ways and in different combinations in different settings. These varia-

tions issue from a number of factors: the disciplinary base of the course, the specific topical or thematic focus of the course, the nature of the institution in which it was offered, the time frame in which it was offered, and the nature of the students involved.

Courses also were developed under this program at Georgetown University, Western Maryland College, and the University of Louisville. They all were solid offerings, but they were sufficiently similar in many respects to those that have been discussed that extensive descriptions of them would seem redundant here. In addition, in all three institutions the courses were passed from one designer/instructor to another, resulting in considerable changes in their syllabi. (This also created difficulties in obtaining solid evaluations of these offerings.) It is possible to contact the institutions to inquire further.

CHAPTER FIVE

INSIGHTS AND OPPORTUNITIES

TEACHING ABOUT
PHILANTHROPY AND VOLUNTARISM

SUGGESTIONS FOR OFFERING COURSES
ABOUT PHILANTHROPY

CIVIC EDUCATION

LIBERAL EDUCATION

CONCLUSION

Our insights from the AAC/AAFRC Program on Studying Philanthropy fall into three categories:

☐ the value of and approaches to teaching about philanthropy and voluntarism in the undergraduate curriculum

☐ possibilities for revitalizing the emphasis on civic education within collegiate education

☐ opportunities for strengthening undergraduate and liberal education more generally.

TEACHING ABOUT PHILANTHROPY AND VOLUNTARISM

The basic questions the AAC/AAFRC program set out to explore were, "Are courses about philanthropy appropri-

ate for an undergraduate liberal arts curriculum? Can they be offered successfully in such a curriculum?" This experiment demonstrates that they are and they can. These courses' intrinsic quality, acceptance by faculty members and administrators, and extraordinary value for the students who took them all demonstrate that teaching about philanthropy is an appropriate focus for courses and portions of courses in undergraduate liberal arts education.

These courses have done exactly what the AAFRC Trust intended, albeit for a limited number of students. They have helped undergraduates learn about what has been and continues to be an important aspect of public and private life in the United States: namely, philanthropic prac-

Both the quality of teaching
and the institutional context
were absolutely crucial
to the success of these courses

tice and voluntary association. The practices of philanthropy and voluntarism have played crucial roles in shaping the character of this nation; the students who have taken these courses will have a far better comprehension of their own society because of this experience.

These courses also contribute to students' gaining a deeper understanding of (at least) one of the fields in the arts and sciences. For example, in courses at Babson College, CUNY–Baruch College, Chapman College, Regis College, and Tufts University—as well as in others—it is clear that students have emerged with a firmer and clearer grasp of key elements and principles of American literature and history, social history, philosophy, economic history, and sociology, respectively. Indeed, as courses intended to enrich students' comprehension of essential facets of these fields, these offerings may be far superior to many more conventional courses; they not only articulated key concepts but also deepened students' interest in these concepts by demonstrating how they were of value in dealing with concrete situations and how they related to students' own experiences.

Courses like these also contribute to the development of students' abilities to see things in a broader perspective, to know how to bring to bear a wide range of knowledge and

ideas in looking at specific questions. A number of these courses succeeded in developing and evoking just that response from the students—perhaps especially those that were intended as senior or "capstone" seminars. For example, one of the reasons the course at Northwestern University has thrived is that philanthropy offers an ideal area of study for a course intended specifically to be an integrative, capstone experience in the liberal arts. That seminar brings together seniors from many different departments to look at a particular set of social issues and practices. It then becomes an occasion for students to contribute to the discussion from their understanding of their own discipline or field of study; at the same time, they can appreciate how the questions under discussion can be understood in a different light from the perspectives of other disciplines.

The fact is that these courses did—and, as many continue to be offered, still do—serve to nurture and develop in students all three of the capacities which we suggested earlier should be essential outcomes of liberal learning and which are capacities necessary for active and constructive citizenship. The ability to think integratively as well as analytically; the ability and inclination to care about what one is learning about and think critically about what one cares about;

and the ability to see the connections between what we know and what we do, to learn from our experience as well as act on our knowledge: these are capacities that clearly were enhanced by students' participation in courses on philanthropy and voluntarism. Any course that strengthens any one of these three kinds of learning—let alone all three—is a course of genuine value in the curriculum.

SUGGESTIONS FOR OFFERING COURSES ABOUT PHILANTHROPY

Two things stood out in the evaluation of the AAC/AAFRC project: Both the quality of teaching and the character of the institutional context were absolutely crucial to the success of these courses. Faculty members interested in developing courses like these on their own campuses must keep these factors in mind. We will say just a few words here about how they should be considered in institutional planning.

The first recommendation is obvious, though it may be difficult to implement. That is, if one wants to launch a course like this, find a great teacher to get it started. The dean of the School of Public Administration at the University of Southern California put the case simply when he told us, "Courses like this live or die according to the quality of the instruction." Certainly, a large measure of the credit for the success of the AAC/AAFRC project is due to the extraordinarily fine teachers who developed and offered these courses. These courses succeed when they are taught by people who are committed to engaging their students in an active learning process and who are willing to become learners with students, seeing new ideas and new connections between ideas emerge from a process of study, dialogue, experience, and reflection.

In the matter of institutional context, the ideal is a situation where there is philosophical and structural support for interdisciplinary scholarship and teaching, where there is acceptance of the legitimacy of experiential learning, and where there is a strong "service ethos" on the campus. Unfortunately, situations where this ideal prevails are rare. Thus, the key to success is adaptation—making the best of those positive elements that do exist.

For instance, it may be difficult to include a service learning component where there is no existing community service network through which one can arrange placements. Professors who must find and screen possible placement sites as well as design and teach the course usually face an impossible work load. There may be a number of options, however, for arranging and overseeing placements other than a campus-based, student service network. Sometimes there are community-based volunteer clearinghouses that can help; even the local United Way may be a resource.

Where either the time frame of the course or the circumstances or work loads of the students make fieldwork an impossibility, there can be other ways to establish the classroom-community connection that was so important and powerful in the pedagogical structure of many of these courses. For example, at Chapman College the use of guest speakers whose presentations have a personal, experiential focus, and who are available to the students for informal discussion, make this connection. Remember also the extremely effective approach to this problem employed at CUNY–Baruch College, where students used their day-to-day lives as the experiential base for the course.

At Seton Hall University, where no supportive structures for interdisciplinary course offerings exist, the interdisciplinary facet of the course is succcessfully implemented through the use of team teaching. At several institutions where team teaching has not been not an option, professors from other departments have been willing to come

into classes as guest lecturers, thereby establishing some opportunities to create an interdisciplinary dialogue that can include the students. Students from different majors who are engaged fully in an active learning process also can create that interdisciplinary conversation.

Finally, even where there is no evident "service ethos" on the campus, many students have been and continue to be involved in voluntary service activity; this is experience that such courses can build on. Data from a variety of sources indicate that between one-half and three-quarters of the students on most campuses will have experience as volunteers, and most of those will be involved in service activities during their college years.[42] One of the reasons most frequently given by students for choosing these courses was that they had been involved in such activity and now wanted to learn more about the larger tradition or organizations of which this activity was a part.

Thus, there are many ways to adapt to a less-than-ideal environment for these kinds of courses, and there probably are more positive factors to work with and build on than may be immediately apparent.

It is important to remember that where the campus environment does not seem favorable in these respects, offering such courses may serve as a catalyst in changing that environment. Offering carefully designed courses that involve experiential and service learning components may help create new and positive connections to the surrounding community for both students and faculty members.[43] The administrator at one institution valued the interdisciplinary character of a course on philanthropy because it helped make other faculty members more aware of the useful possibilities for interdisciplinary scholarship and instruction. We also were struck by the many administrators who valued having these courses in their curriculum as signs that their institutions wanted more attention to be given to issues and activities of community service.[44]

Obviously, we are affirming the value of courses about philanthropy. We urge interested faculty members and administrators to consider the possibilities for developing such courses on their campuses. The suggestions above may be taken as cautions about factors to consider before offering such courses; we hope they also will be taken as encouragements to initiate courses like those in the AAC/AAFRC project that have been so useful to students and institutions.

CIVIC EDUCATION

We argued at some length in Chapter Two that it is very important for institutions of higher education to concern themselves again with the work of civic education. This has been part of their traditional mission, and clearly it is still part of the public's expectation of them. Most colleges and universities at least pay lip service to the legitimacy of this claim in their mission statements or catalogues. It also is true, however, that most institutions in fact do little to address this need for preparing their students to be more active and constructive members of their communities.

There is likely to be continuing and growing distress among the public over this failure on the part of these institutions—who are, after all, supposed to be serving the public good in this way as well as in others. Failure to prepare graduates to be creative and responsible members of a democratic society will not only contribute to the continuing erosion of civic life but also, eventually, will have a direct and dramatic impact on these same institutions—for institutions committed to unfettered inquiry and a free exchange of ideas will not long survive in a society where larger democratic ideals are not affirmed in principle and practice.

Attending to civic education
does not have to mean
the addition of new programs
in the curriculum

Attending to the need for civic education does not have to mean the addition of new programs in the curriculum. Rather, broadening the possibilities for the subjects we teach and teaching in different ways can go a long way toward attaining this goal. We have tried to demonstrate how these courses on philanthropy illustrate the possibilities by bringing into the curriculum a subject that invites students to think integratively as well as analytically, make connections between academic study and life experience, and see how the knowledge they gain brings with it both the power and the responsibility to act. Certainly, other subjects may be taught in ways that serve these purposes as well, but courses and teaching about philanthropy may be a particularly useful vehicle in this regard.

Finally, we have argued that the intellectual capacities and personal attributes that undergird good citizenship ought to be among the basic outcomes of a liberal education in any case. Thus, giving more attention to developing these skills and characteristics in students does not divert time and energy from more important goals of undergraduate education; rather, it focuses some of that time and energy more productively. This highlights opportunities our experience with this program tells us may exist for enhancing the quality of liberal education more generally.

LIBERAL EDUCATION

One of the common factors distinguishing the courses in the AAC/AAFRC Program on Studying Philanthropy from many other courses the students involved had taken previously was the intensity and quality of the learning they experienced. Many of these students said that these were the best courses they had ever taken or that they expected to remember and use what they learned in these courses well beyond what they remembered or used from other courses. Our conversations with and observations of these students indicate these claims have merit. A few students, as we have indicated, described these courses as experiences that changed their fundamental perspectives or brought them into whole new ways—usually, more wholistic ways—of thinking.

Being confronted with so many emphatic responses has caused us to look long and hard at what was so special about these offerings. We have concluded there were two elements that made a difference, and these are elements of course design and pedagogy that often could be incorporated into other liberal arts courses to enrich them as learning experiences for students. One is an interdisciplinary aspect; the other is a component of experiential learning and reflection.

It probably would not be possible, and almost certainly not be desirable, to make every course interdisciplinary. At the early stages of students' college careers—ironically, when they do most of their work in general education and so are most likely to be exposed to multidisciplinary courses—most truly interdisciplinary courses are likely to be of little value because students do not have sufficient grounding in any discipline or field to do meaningful comparative studies.

Yet it also is true that most college students graduate without ever having had an opportunity to develop any critical perspective about the limitations of the understandings and modes of inquiry of whatever discipline or field they major in. Surely this is one of the reasons so many supposedly "well-educated" policy makers appear to understand only one narrow, specialized way of viewing a problem and miss even seeing many significant factors that should be considered.

Genuine interdisciplinary study offers students one way to get past this narrowness and develop critical perspective on their own fields. Requiring interdisciplinary study is one way to ensure that college grad-uates are truly well-educated. It would make students more likely to go forth into society with some of the tolerance for ambiguity, respect for other views, and willingness to learn from people different from themselves which are essential qualities of those who will be involved constructively in civic life. As a recent AAC report put it, "We are educated in this world to the degree that we are aware of our own boundedness and partiality, and that we become skilled in seeking out, understanding, and integrating the perspectives of others."[45]

Because well-structured interdisciplinary study develops these skills, it should be part of every program of liberal education. It also is immensely appealing; a great many of the students in these courses said that the chance to be part of an interdisciplinary course was one of the things that attracted them to the courses and one of the elements of the courses they found most exciting.

The other factor that made many of these courses so powerful for students was the inclusion of an experiential learning component. When most people think about the liberal arts the first things that come to their minds are books and lectures; the last thing that comes to mind is fieldwork. There is ample evidence, however, that the most effective forms of teaching involve fieldwork or experience combined with reflection as well as study. The prejudice against experiential learning in the liberal arts has its roots in historically conditioned views of the value of theory over practice that are too seldom critically examined.[46]

We have cited many of the comments of students in these courses about the value of the experiential components for "making things real," helping them understand "the meaning and significance" of ideas presented in readings or classes, and more generally bringing them into an active rather than a passive mode as learners. Students repeatedly spoke of the power of the interplay among the courses' academic components (reading, lectures, discussions), experiential elements, and occasions for reflection. These experiences are predicted, or at least explained, by the work of educational theorists like David Kolb and social scientists like Fred Emory.[47] What becomes abundantly clear in our interviews with these students is how much their learning experience in these courses was enriched by this combination of pedagogical elements.

We are left to wonder how many other kinds of liberal arts courses—not just those about philanthropy or social issues—might be enriched by the creative inclusion of experi-

ential elements. We strongly urge faculty members in the liberal arts to consider these possibilities. They might find that including such components would not dilute the important disciplinary focus of their courses but instead might make the central concepts and approaches to inquiry they are trying to convey more accesible and meaningful for their students.

CONCLUSION

Finally, then, we urge others to consider philanthropy as an area of study for the undergraduate curriculum. Our experience is that courses about philanthropy may serve a number of valuable and important purposes.

☐ They teach undergraduates about an important element of American history and culture that students must understand better to understand their own society.

☐ These courses also can become excellent vehicles for reengaging colleges and universities in the work of civic education—once an important part of their mission.

☐ They can, by the same measure, become important vehicles for helping students develop those intellectual capacities and personal attributes that should mark people who have experienced a truly liberal education.

We hope that the material presented here has helped convince the reader that the study of philanthropy belongs in the undergraduate liberal arts curriculum. We also hope it will offer those who might be interested in developing courses like those in the AAC/AAFRC Program on Studying Philanthropy the

encouragement and ideas to get started. Finally, we hope that the discussion of AAC's goals and efforts in this project may stimulate more dialogue and action addressing opportunities to enrich the quality of undergraduate education that our work in this project has revealed.

MODEL COURSES: ABBREVIATED SYLLABI

"Voluntary Association, Philanthropy, and Community in American Culture"
(an American studies seminar)

Learning Goals
The purpose of this course is to help students understand the special roles that the practices of voluntary association and philanthropy have played in shaping American society. It will focus especially on the persistent tensions between the value American culture traditionally has placed on individualism and self-sufficiency, on the one hand, and on community and generosity of spirit, on the other.

This society gives great weight to ideals of individual acheivement and success, yet it also has seen itself as a nation in terms of cultural images like "a city on the hill" and a society of "caring communities." What have been the functions of philanthropic practice and voluntary association in resolving or sustaining the tensions between these ideals? Are we seeing the balance between these ideals break down in favor of the values of individualism in recent years?

Course Structure
This is a seminar requiring extensive reading and full participation in discussions by all students. In addition, each student will be required to complete a field research project focusing on a voluntary organization and its role in its local community. Students will prepare a reflective paper reporting on their findings and relating them to the issues discussed in class and make a presentation to the seminar on their work. Students will be evaluated on their participation in the seminar, their research work, and two short papers responding to particular readings.

LEARNING
FOR THE
COMMON GOOD

Texts
Readings will include *Habits of the Heart*, by Robert Bellah, et al.; *American Philanthropy*, by Robert Bremner; excerpts from *America's Voluntary Spirit* (*AVS*), by Brian O'Connell (ed.); *The Blithedale Romance*, by Nathaniel Hawthorne; and *Up From Slavery*, by Booker T. Washington.

Seminar Topics
Seminar sessions will be organized around explorations of the following topics:
1. Individualism and the Search for Community: readings include *Habits of the Heart* and excerpts from *AVS* (Winthrop, Mather, and de Tocqueville)
2. The Romance of Community: readings include *The Blithdale Romance* and excerpts from *AVS* (Emerson, Thoreau, and Schlesinger)
3. The Development of American Philanthropy: readings include *American Philanthropy* and excerpts from *AVS* (Cass & Manser, Rockefeller, Boorstin, and Curti)
4. Philanthropy, Advocacy, and Social Reform: readings include *Up From Slavery* and excerpts from *AVS* (Addams, Bethune, Eisenberg, Smith, and Lyman)

"Giving, Serving, and Self-Fulfillment:
An Inquiry into the Ethics of Philanthropy"
(a philosophy course)

Learning Goals
This course will lead students into an examination of the practice of philanthropy from a philosophical and ethical perspective. Insofar as all efforts in giving and serving are, in principle, efforts "to do good," it is important to ask why people undertake such efforts and what "good" is ultimately achieved —and for whom—in such efforts.

Can people do the right things for the wrong reasons? Should it make any difference what motivates giving or service so long as those in need are really served? And what are the benefits to the giver of engaging in philanthropic activity? These are among the key questions this course will explore.

Course Structure
Students will be required to do extensive reading and participate fully in class discussions. There will be several guest speakers, including people who are active in philanthropic service. Students will be required to write two short papers (3–5 pages each) reflecting on some of the readings and speakers. Each student will develop an in-depth profile of one living philanthropist/volunteer in their own community, a process which should include interviewing that person about their motivations for and experiences with giving and serving. Each student will give a brief presentation of that profile to the class in the last half of the semester and submit the full profile in writing. There will be a final, comprehensive, take-home exam.

Texts
Readings will include: *Vice and Virtue in Everyday Life* (VV), Christina Hoff Sommers (ed.); *On Caring*, Milton Mayerhoff; *A Burnt-Out Case*, Graham Greene; and *America's Voluntary Spirit* (AVS), Brian O'Connell (ed.). There also will be numerous library and photocopied pieces.

Class Topics
Class sessions will be organized around consideration of the following themes:
1. Morality, Self-Interest, and Egoism: readings include excerpts from AVS (Marts, pages 143–51; O'Connell, 407–8) and VV (Rachels, 97–110; Lasch, 427–36; Sommers, 623–27)
2. The Religious and Historical Roots of Philanthropy: readings include "Philanthropic Values" by Robert Payton and excerpts from AVS (the Bible, Weaver, and Winthrop)
3. Theories of Right Action: readings include "Utilitarianism," Mill (VV, 79–85); "Good Will, Duty, and the Categorical Imperative," Kant (VV, 86–96); "The Gospel of Wealth," Carnegie (AVS, 97–108)
4. Applying the Theories to World Hunger: readings include excerpts from VV (Singer and Hardin, 590–613) and "To Relieve Human Misery," Brian O'Connell, from *Philanthropy in Action*
5. Virtue Ethics: readings include excerpts from VV (Gansberg, 35–39; Taylor, 40–52; Mayo, 171–76; Aristotle, 148–58)
6. Caring and Generosity: readings include Mayerhoff, *On Caring*, 1–40; "Generosity," Wallace, (VV, 216–23)
7. Self-Respect and Love: readings will include biographical material on

Eleanor Roosevelt; "Achieving Civil Rights," Franklin (*AVS*); and excerpts
from *VV* (Theroux, 286–87; Kant, 390–94; Didion, 409–14)
8. Caring and Gratitude: readings include *On Caring*, 41–87, and excerpts
from *VV* (Berger, 193–208; English, 460–67).
9. Women's Roles: readings include excerpts from *AVS* (Addams, 73–80;
Dodd, 155–59); from *The Woman's Bible*, Stanton; the report of the "NOW
Task Force on Voluntarism" (1975)
10. Service and Vocations/Honesty with Oneself: readings include Greene, *A
Burnt-Out Case*, 7–78; excerpts from *VV* (Johnson, 260–63; Butler, 264–70)
11. Service and Vocation/Altruism in Health Care: readings include *A Burnt-
Out Case*, 79–199; "Altruism in Health Care," by Green (in the library)
12. Voluntarism and Philanthropy Organized: readings include excerpts from
AVS (de Tocqueville, 53–57; Curti, 161–75; "The Filer Commission," 299–313;
Nielsen, 363–69)
13. Ethics and Fund-raising: readings include excerpts from *AVS* (McGuffey's
Reader, 59–61; Washington, 63–71; Thoreau, 91–95)

"American Philanthropy: Past and Present"
(a history course)

Learning Goals
The purpose of this course is to help students understand the very important role philanthropy and voluntarism has played in shaping American society, how that role developed and changed over time, and how our society
now is influenced by individual philanthropy and philanthropic organizations. This will involve the students in an examination of the religious and
philosophical roots of philanthropic practice, the political and economic
forces that have shaped that practice (and been shaped by it) in the development of the United States, and the ways philanthropic organizations have
interacted with government and business.

Course Structure
This course encompasses traditional academic study, field research, and service. Students are expected to do all the readings and to write three short reflective papers on particular pieces of their choice. They also are expected to
write a history of a local voluntary or philanthropic organization of their
choice. This will involve talking with persons involved with that organiza-

tion and reviewing its records, as well as reading about it. Students also are expected to volunteer with a voluntary organization—putting in forty-five hours over the course of the semester—to get a feel for how such organizations function. (We would suggest they may find it advantageous to volunteer for the organization they are going to study.) Over the duration of the term we also will host several guest speakers in the class who will talk about the history and present work of philanthropic organizations they know first-hand.

Texts
Readings for this course include: *American Philanthropy*, by Robert Bremner; *America's Voluntary Spirit* (AVS), by Brian O'Connell (ed.); *The Third America*, by Michael O'Neill; and excerpts from other works.

Class Topics
Class sessions will be organized around consideration of the following topics:
1. The Origins of Philanthropy: readings include "Philanthropic Values," by Robert Payton; and excerpts from AVS (pages 1–23)
2. The Beginnings of Philanthropy in America: readings include *American Philanthropy*, 1–39; excerpts from AVS (Winthrop, 29–34; Mather, 45–48)
3. Benevolence and Voluntarism in the Young Republic: readings include *American Philanthropy*, 40–54; excerpts from AVS (Emerson, de Tocqueville, and Thoreau; 49–58 and 91–97)
4. The Effects of War: readings include *American Philanthropy*, 55–84
5. "Scientific Philanthropy": readings include *American Philanthropy*, 85–115; "A Bridge Founded Upon Justice and Built of Human Hearts," Peter Dobkin Hall
6. From Charity to Philanthropy: readings include excerpts from AVS (Carnegie, Rockefeller, Rosenwald, and Boorstin; 97–144) and a case study on the Moorestown Female Charitable Society
7. The Birth of Modern Philanthropy and Fund-raising: readings include *American Philanthropy*, 116–35; a case study on "The Transformation of the YMCA," Mayer and Zald
8. Philanthropy, the Depression, and a Key Transition: readings include *American Philanthropy*, 136–55
9. Philanthropy in the Modern World: readings include *American Philanthropy*, 156–216
10. Women in Philanthropy: readings include excerpts from AVS (Addams,

73–80; Dodd, 155–60); the Report of the NOW Task Force on Voluntarism (1975); "Participation, Leadership, and the Role of Voluntarism among Selected Women Volunteers," Jessica Reynolds Jenner
11. Philanthropy and Diversity in American Culture: readings from the *Foundation News* issue on "Pluralism in Philanthropy" (1990)
12. Contemporary Philanthropy/Religion, Education, and Culture: readings from *The Third America* (chapters 1, 2, 3, and 5)
13. Contemporary Philanthropy/Health Care and Social Services: readings from *The Third America* (chapters 4, 6 and 7)
14. Contemporary Philanthropy/Foundations and Mutual Benefit Organizations: readings from *The Third America* (chapters 9 and 10)

"Philanthropy and Community"
(a sociology course)

Learning Goals
This course explores the culture, history, social organization, and political economy of philanthropy in the United States. It will focus special attention on the ways issues of class, race, gender, and ethnicity are reflected in and affected by philanthropic activity. It centers around considerations of the nature of "community" as people's experience of the elements of life and society that bind them together and looks at the way practices of giving and volunteering reinforce those bonds, for better and for worse.

Course Structure
Requirements for this course include participation in a community service project, readings and participation in class discussion, and producing several short papers in reaction to the readings and class discussion. Students also will be expected to keep a journal in which they reflect and comment upon their reactions to and learning from all these activities. (The journals will be reviewed but not graded.)

Texts
Readings include: *Habits of the Heart*, by Robert Bellah, et al.; *American Philanthropy*, by Robert Bremner; *Free Spaces: The Sources of Democratic Change in America*, by Sara Evans and Harry Boyte (out of print; on reserve in library); and other materials to be made available.

Class Topics
Course sessions will be organized around the following themes:
1. Different Images of Philanthropy and Voluntarism, with specific focus on:
   a) Philanthropy and Dimensions of Socioeconomic Class
   b) Women, Philanthropy, and Voluntarism
   c) African Americans and Philanthropy
2. Voluntary Action, Social Movements, and Social Space: readings from Evans and Boyte (chapters 1, 4 and 6)
3. Individualism, Commitment, and Community: readings from Bellah, et al. (Introduction and chapters 6, 7, 8 and 10)
4. Voluntary Action and Government
5. Philanthropy, Voluntarism, Social Structure, and the Market Economy
6. The Structure and Dynamics of Voluntary Giving of Time and Money, with a specific focus on:
   a) Volunteering in Community Service Organizations
   b) Working for Pay in Nonprofit Organizations
   c) Foundations and Their Impact
   d) Corporate Philanthropy and Social Responsibility
7. Connecting Theory and Practice: students report on their field projects

"The Nonprofit Sector and the Public Good"
(an interdisciplinary public policy course)

Learning Goals
This course is designed to introduce students to American political institutions and processes by focusing on the role of the nonprofit sector in American public life. Historically, nongovernmental nonprofit organizations created to serve public purposes have played major roles in shaping the American political economy; as the needs and problems of society have shifted, however, the roles and relationships of nonprofits, government, and business have shifted as well. At the conclusion of this course, students should understand how the nonprofit sector developed and how its role in society changed and evolved over time; they also should see how it interacts with government and business to shape American society as we know it today.

Course Structure
This course integrates readings from a variety of social sciences with the student's fieldwork. Students will be expected to complete all readings and participate in class discussions. There will be a midterm and a final examination. Finally, students will be expected to work with a local voluntary organization and develop a study of that organization that examines the ways it functions to serve both public and private interests. Students will make a presentation to the class as well as prepare a paper on their findings. Professors will lecture on important concepts and material, and there will be guest speakers, in addition to the presentation of information through the readings.

Texts
Readings will include: *American Philanthropy*, by Robert Bremner; *Free Spaces*, by Sara Evans and Harry Boyte (out of print; on reserve in library); *The Nonprofit Sector: A Research Handbook* (*TNS*), by Walter Powell (ed.); and *America's Voluntary Spirit* (*AVS*), by Brian O'Connell (ed.). There will be additional readings provided.

Class Topics
Class sessions will be organized around consideration of the following topics:
1. Definitions, Dimensions, and Boundaries of the Nonprofit Sector: readings include excerpts from *AVS* ("The Filer Commission," pages 287–313; Smith, 331–44) and "The Scope and Dimensions of Nonprofit Activity" (*TNS*, 55–66)
2. Historical Perspectives: readings from *American Philanthropy*, with session and readings specifically focused on:
   a) the colonial period to the mid-nineteenth century
   b) industrialization to the 1920s
   c) the Great Depression to the 1980s
3. Preparation for field study
4. Government and the Market: readings include "Economic Theories of Nonprofit Organizations" (*TNS*, 27–41)
5. Nonprofits, Government, and Business: readings include excerpts from *TNS* (Douglas, 43–54; Salamon, 99–117)
6. Charitable Behavior: readings from the *Nonprofit and Voluntary Sector Quarterly* and the *Journal of Voluntary Action Research*; and from *TNS* (Jencks, 321–39)

7. Federated Funding Organizations: readings to be provided

8. Commercial Enterprises, Government Contracts, and Nonprofits: reading from TNS (Skloot, 380–96)

9. Foundation and Corporate Philanthropy: readings include excerpts from AVS (Gardner, 255–62; Karl, 376–83); TNS (Useem, 340–359; Ylvisaker, 360–79).

10. Case studies focused specifically on:

   a) Health Care: reading from TNS (Marmor, 221–39)

   b) Social Welfare: reading from TNS (Kramer, 258–76)

   c) Advocacy and Social Reform: readings include Free Spaces, by Evans and Boyte (on reserve); "Nonprofit Organizations and Policy Advocacy" (TNS, 296–318)

   d) The Arts: reading from TNS (DiMaggio, 195–220)

11. Presentations of field studies

◆ ◆ ◆

These model syllabi draw on many of the best features of a number of courses developed in the AAC/AAFRC Program on Studying Philanthropy. Four of these course outlines, however, follow particularly closely the designs of specific courses in AAC's project.

The American studies seminar that begins this appendix is based largely on the course designed by Fritz Fleischmann at Babson College. The philosophy course that follows reflects the design of Mike W. Martin's course at Chapman College.

The sociology course syllabus draws heavily upon the offering created by Susan Ostrander at Tufts University.

Where readings are not suggested here, it is because she uses an extensive collection of articles from many sources—far more citations than we can provide in this limited space. She may be contacted directly for more information.

Finally, for the design of the interdisciplinary public policy seminar we are indebted to Richard Sundeen and James Ferris of the University of Southern California. They also use extensive additional readings, and they may be contacted for a complete list of those resources.

We are especially grateful to the faculty members who developed and taught these courses.

∎

SELECTED RESOURCES

Philanthropy, voluntarism, and the nonprofit sector

Bellah, Robert N., et al. *Habits of the Heart: Individualism and Commitment in American Life.* Berkeley: University of California Press, 1985.

A landmark study of the tension between the values of individualism and community in American life; this book can be very useful in raising those issues, but it may be very difficult reading for many undergraduates.

Bremner, Robert H. *American Philanthropy*, 2nd ed. Chicago: University of Chicago Press, 1988.

A solid, comprehensive, and very readable history of the practice of philanthropy in the United States. This is an excellent basic text for providing an historical overview.

Ellis, Susan J., and Katherine Noyes. *By the People: A History of Americans as Volunteers.* San Francisco: Jossey-Bass, 1990.

Another solid and useful history; this one focuses specifically on the traditions and practices of voluntary association and voluntary service and their roles in shaping American society.

Hodgkinson, Virginia A., and Murray S. Weitzman. *Dimensions of the Independent Sector.* Washington: Independent Sector, 1990.

This volume provides a remarkably comprehensive and detailed statistical profile of the third sector as it presently is constituted. It includes extensive information on the numbers and types of organizations and volunteers as well as the sources and uses of financial support. It is a very useful resource book for people teaching courses with a contemporary focus and an emphasis on the economics, politics, organization, and operations of the sector.

James, Estelle, and Susan Rose-Ackerman *The Nonprofit Enterprise in Market Economics.* London: Harwood Academic Publishers, 1986.

A brief, very helpful, and very accessible (even to a non-economist) introduction to the economic principles and dynamics of nonprofit and philanthropic activity.

Liberal Education (September/October 1988).

This issue of AAC's bimonthly journal focuses on teaching about philanthropy and voluntarism. The Praxis section includes descriptions of several of the courses in the AAC/AAFRC Program on Studying Philanthropy. (The Praxis section of the September/October 1989 issue includes descriptions of several more of these courses.)

O'Connell, Brian, ed. *America's Voluntary Spirit*. New York: The Foundation Center, 1983.

The best available collection of readings from primary sources about philanthropy, voluntarism, and the nonprofit sector.

Odenhal, Theresa J. *Charity Begins at Home*. New York: Basic Books, 1990.

A very important study of the role of philanthropy in protecting the interests of the privileged, this could well be used to raise a critical perspective on the practice of philanthropy.

O'Neill, Michael. *The Third America*. San Francisco: Jossey-Bass, 1989.

A useful and simple overview of the nonprofit sector, its history and present contours. Good for helping students gain perspective on the sector, though for use in a class it needs to be balanced by more critical material.

Payton, Robert L. *Philanthropy: Voluntary Action for the Public Good*. New York: Macmillan, 1988.

A wonderful collection of writings about philanthropy and potentially a useful source of readings for undergraduate courses.

_____. "Philanthropic Values." In *Philanthropy: Private Means, Public Ends*, edited by Kenneth W. Thompson. Lanham, Md.: University Press of America, 1987.

Probably the best single essay on the religious, philosophical, and historical origins and development of philanthropy; this is a great introductory piece for courses about philanthropy.

Powell, Walter W., ed. *The Nonprofit Sector: A Research Handbook*. New Haven: Yale University Press, 1987.

An invaluable collection of pieces providing background on the central elements, issues, and concerns of the nonprofit sector.

Van Til, John. *Mapping the Third Sector*. New Brunswick, N.J.: Transaction Press, 1987.

This is a detailed and comprehensive analysis of the origins and social, economic, and political facets of the nonprofit sector and its relation to the larger political economy. While offering a thorough overview, this may be difficult reading for many undergraduates.

Working Papers from the Spring Research Forums. Washington: Independent Sector, 1983–1991.

These volumes are collections of working papers presented annually (there is a separate volume for each year) to a conference of scholars and practitioners studying and working with philanthropy and nonprofit organizations. They contain many pieces that could be useful in presenting specific topics in undergraduate courses.

The Nonprofit and Voluntary Sector Quarterly. San Francisco: Jossey-Bass.

This is a quarterly publication of the Association for Research on Nonprofit Organizations and Voluntary Action. Prior to 1989 it was *The Journal for Voluntary Action Research*. This may be a good source of readings for courses on philanthropy and voluntarism.

Finally, two bibliographies list other materials about philanthropy, voluntarism, and the nonprofit sector. Both are published by the Foundation Center in New York:

☐ *Philanthropy and Voluntarism: An Annotated Bibliography* (1987), by Daphne N. Layton. This bibliography was produced as part of AAC's Program on Studying Philanthropy.

☐ *The Literature of the Nonprofit Sector* (1990)

Integrating service or work experience with course work and academic learning

Johnson Foundation. *Principles of Good Practice for Combining Service and Learning*. Racine, Wisc.: Johnson Foundation, 1989.

This pamphlet is the product of a Wingspread Conference and is an essential resource for those interested in service learning. It offers and explains some fundamental guidelines for setting up, running, and evaluating service-learning programs.

Kendall, Jane C., et al. *Combining Service and Learning: A Resource Book for Community and Public Service*. Raleigh, N.C.: National Society for Internships and Experiential Education, 1990.

This three-volume set contains excellent articles touching on virtually every aspect, practical and theoretical, of experiential and service learning. It offers profiles of model programs and provides a comprehensive bibliography of additional resources.

Civic education and higher education

Morse, Suzanne W. *Renewing Civic Capacity: Preparing College Students for Service and Citizenship*. ASHE-ERIC Higher Education Report #8. Washington: American Society for Higher Education, 1989.

This monograph offers a comprehensive review of the history of American higher education's involvement with citizenship education, as well as a careful analysis of the reasons it is important to renew attention to this work and how that might be done. The references will steer interested parties to many other resources as well.

The Civic Arts Review

This is a quarterly publication of the Arneson Institute of Ohio Wesleyan University. It regularly offers helpful essays, articles, and interviews relating liberal education to civic education and concerns for public life more broadly.

The Kettering Review. Dayton, Ohio: Kettering Foundation.

This is another quarterly publication. It too provides a wealth of valuable material for those concerned with public life, liberal education, and civic education.

The character and purposes of liberal education

Kimball, Bruce A. *Orators and Philosophers: A History of the Idea of Liberal Education.* New York: Teachers College Press, 1986.

This book offers a very useful presentation and analysis of the ideals and purposes of liberal education, their origins and development, and the ways they have changed in different cultural contexts.

_____. "The Historical and Cultural Dimensions of the Recent Reports on Undergraduate Education." Lecture presented at the Lilly Endowment Workshop on the Liberal Arts, Colorado Springs, 1987.

While referencing and examining a number of reports on the undergraduate curriculum, this lecture provides a briefer and less detailed—but still very useful—review of many of the ideas in *Orators and Philosophers.*

Minnich, Elizabeth K. *Transforming Knowledge.* Philadelphia: Temple University Press, 1990.

Palmer, Parker. *To Know as We Are Known: A Spirituality of Education.* San Francisco: Harper & Row, 1983.

The Challenge of Connecting Learning: Liberal Learning and the Arts and Sciences Major. Washington: Association of American Colleges, 1991.

Integrity in the College Curriculum: A Report to the Academic Community. Washington: AAC, 1985.

Liberal Education is a journal devoted to consideration of topics of interest for undergraduate education in the arts and sciences. It is published five times yearly by the Association of American Colleges.

■

LIST OF COURSES

This listing of the courses developed through the AAC/AAFRC Program on Studying Philanthropy–with the institution, course title, department, and instructor–includes offerings referenced in the text. Note that this list gives the title and instructor of the course as they were during the evaluation visit; in some cases, these courses have changed and now may be offered by other instructors. In most instances, the designer/instructors of these courses can be reached at the institutions listed. In a few cases where professors may have left that institution, it still may be possible to contact the college or university to get more information on that specific course. AAC also is acting as a clearinghouse for information on these courses throughout the 1991–92 academic year.

Two institutions that received grants–Harvard University and Southern University–dropped out of the program when local circumstances made it impossible for them to proceed with their course offerings as specified under the terms of the grant.

Babson College: "Individualism and Philanthropy in American Life" (American studies seminar); Fritz Fleischmann

Chapman College: "A Life of Service" (philosophy course); Mike W. Martin

City University of New York–Bernard Baruch College: "Voluntarism and the Problems of Dependency" (history seminar); David Rosner

Georgetown University: "Philanthropy, Voluntarism, and Public Policy" (government/political science course); Margaret Wyszomirski and Leslie Lenkowsky

Illinois State University: "Voluntary Organizations and Global Development" (political science course); Robert Hunt

Northwestern University: "Philanthropy in America" (interdisciplinary/American studies seminar); Robert Klaus (or contact Carl Smith)

Randolph-Macon Woman's College: "Philanthropy and Volunteer Service in America" (religious studies course); Linda Koch Lorimer and Ivor Thomas

Regis College (Mass.): "Perspectives on American Philanthropy" (economics and history course); Mary Oates

Seton Hall University: "American Philanthropy: Historical and Political Perspectives" (political science course); William Brandon

Temple University: "Voluntarism and Community Organization" (sociology/urban studies course); Ronnie Steinberg

Tufts University: "Philanthropy and Community" (sociology/American studies course); Susan Ostrander

University of Louisville: "Voluntarism" (sociology course); Mark Austin

University of Southern California: "The Nonprofit Sector and the Public Interest" (interdisciplinary/public policy course); James Ferris and Richard Sundeen

Western Maryland College: "Philanthropy and Voluntarism" (history course); Patrick Reed

RESULTS OF STUDENT SURVEY

As part of the evaluation process for the AAC/AAFRC Program on Studying Philanthropy, questionnaires were distributed to participating students in almost every course at the end of each offering. The responses compiled here encompass the first three years of course offerings.

Because there were two rounds of grants, the offerings extended over a four-year period: eight courses from 1987–90 and six from 1988–91. We do not include responses from the fourth year because many had not yet been returned at the time this report was being prepared; in any case, the statistical patterns were extremely consistent over the first three years. (There was no variance exceeding 4 percent in the responses to any item from one year to another.)

Return rates for these questionnaires was 62 percent over the first three years. There were approximately 520 students involved in the courses during that period, of whom 320 returned usable questionnaires to us. (An additional 80 to 90 students were involved in the last year.)

I
DEMOGRAPHICS

Age		Sex	
18	2	Male	125
19	19	Female	193
20	56		
21	134	**Class**	
22	56	Freshmen	4
23	13	Sophomores	27
24	12	Juniors	94
25	6	Seniors	179
26	3	Graduates	13
27	4		
28	2	**Religion**	
29	1	Catholic	124
30	2	Protestant	80
31–35	1	Jewish	22
36–45	5	Other	5
		None	85

Race	
White	282
Black	14
Other	17

II
EXPERIENCE WITH VOLUNTEERING

Students' involvement in volunteering

Yes	262
No	58

Number of hours

3 or less	147
3 to 10	89
More than 10	26

When students were involved in volunteering

In high school	65
In college	56
At other times	17
High school and college	77
High school and other	8
College and other	3
All of the above	36

How students came to be involved in volunteering

Through:	#	%
Civic organizations	9	3
School (and related organizations)	74	28
Religious organizations	26	10
Other (cultural, sports, etc.)	26	10
Civic and school	20	8
Civic and religious	12	5
Civic and other	1	1
School and religious	48	18
School and other	7	3
Religious and other	7	3
Civic, school, and religious	17	7
Civic, school, and other	8	3
School, religious, and other	6	2

(percentage totals more than 100 due to rounding)

Note: The significance of schools and colleges providing students with opportunities for voluntary service seems clear. By far, the largest number of students—69 percent—cited their high school or college as the place where they became involved in volunteering. Only religious institutions—45 percent—came close to involving so many.

III
EXPERIENCE IN COURSEWORK AND FIELDWORK

Students having previous courses in philanthropy

Yes	17*
No	302

*Note: An examination of the descriptions given for most of these courses shows they actually deal with philanthropy or voluntarism only marginally, if at all.

Students' participation included experiential component

Yes	206
No	109

Students' views of the value of experiential components

Not valuable	15
Somewhat valuable	115
Very valuable	184
No opinion	6

Value placed on "fieldwork" component if part of their experience

Not valuable	2
Somewhat valuable	53
Very valuable	150
No opinion	1

Value placed on "fieldwork" component if not part of their experience

Not valuable	13
Somewhat valuable	52
Very valuable	34
No opinion	10

Note: We were struck by the high value students placed on including experiential elements in these courses. Almost 60 percent of all students responding thought including these elements was (or should be) "very valuable." Even for those for whom this was not a part of their course, almost 80 percent believed it would have been at least "somewhat valuable." For those for whom it was part of the course, this experience confirmed their view of the power of experiential learning, with the percentage of those rating this as "very valuable" climbing to 74 percent.

IV
EXPECTATIONS

Taking the course will affect student's choices of future studies

Yes	158
No	57
Unsure	102

Note: Most of those who said yes—and a number of those who said they were unsure—indicated that the course they had taken had stimulated their interest in the subjects of philanthropy, voluntarism, nonprofit organizations, or social welfare. Many of those who said they were unsure how this would affect their choices of future studies suggested that this was because they did not know where or if they could find other courses on these subjects.

Taking the course will affect choices of future careers

Yes	169
No	58
Unsure	90

Note: Most of the students giving positive responses here say that, being more aware of the role and activities of the nonprofit sector and voluntary organizations, they now would be more interested in considering employment in the sector. Very few indicate any commitment to that as a career path.

Will affect choices of future activities

Yes	218
No	38
Unsure	60

Note: Given the opportunity to explain this response, 202 of the 218 students responding positively said that they will be more involved in some form of voluntarism or philanthropy, or that they are committed to continuing the considerable involvement they now maintain, because of what they learned in these courses. Some of those who said "no" indicated that this was because they already were involved and intended to stay active. Reflecting the critical stance these courses tried to maintain, five of the students who said their future activities will be affected indicated that they will be more reluctant to donate money or get involved because of what they have learned.

NOTES

Introduction

1. Only 17 of 320 students (5 percent) responding to our survey said that they previously had "any coursework relating to this subject." (See Appendix D, pages 75–78, for a complete summary of the results of the surveys of students participating in these courses.) Many of those we interviewed said they had "no understanding" of what philanthropy was prior to taking one of these courses. In fact, simple curiosity about what philanthropy meant often was given as one of the reasons for taking these courses.

2. At least 58 percent of the students in courses developed through the AAC project had been involved in voluntary service prior to enrolling in the classes. (The 58 percent figure includes only those who said they were involved in volunteering in high school. Up to 82 percent may have been involved in volunteering for the first time as part of these courses. See Appendix D, page 76.)

This correlates with the results of a 1990 Independent Sector survey of adolescents which showed that 58 percent of teens were involved in volunteering, averaging 3.9 hours per week of service. In addition, several admissions officers we interviewed at participating colleges and universities said "at least two-thirds" of their incoming students have experience in volunteer service.

3. Our thinking in this regard has been reinforced and enriched by the address on "The Future of Civic Education" that Elizabeth Minnich gave to AAC's conference on "Collegiate Education and the Cultivation of Civic Consciousness" in Chicago, April 13, 1991. The conference was an outgrowth of AAC's Program on Studying Philanthropy.

Chapter 1. Background

4. Quoted in Robert H. Bremner, *American Philanthropy* (Chicago: University of Chicago Press, 1988), 115.

5. I am indebted here and in the discussion that follows to the very useful history of the tradition of liberal education provided by Bruce Kimball in "The Historical and Cultural Dimensions of the Recent Reports on Undergraduate Education" (Lecture to the Lilly Endowment Workshop on the Liberal Arts, 1987), as well as in his book *Orators and Philosophers: A History of the Idea of Liberal Education* (New York: Teachers College Press, 1986).

6. Bernard Murchland, "Civic Education—by Default," *The Kettering Review* (December 1990), 13.

7. Obviously, there are exceptions to this observation. Nevertheless, our own survey of four-year institutions, and those of others, indicates the general validity of this point. In our survey of 414 institutions (representing all types of undergraduate colleges and universities, conducted in the spring of 1990), 67 percent said they thought "work or service activities combined with study, discussion, and/or opportunities for reflection" represent the most effective way of providing "civic education"; only 15 percent could say they involved their students in such a combination of activities, however. Asked whether they needed "to improve their efforts to prepare students for citizenship," 53 percent "strongly agreed" and another 43 percent "agreed" that they did.

8. Kimball, "Historical and Cultural Dimensions of Recent Reports," 17.

Chapter 2. Civic Education and Liberal Education

9. Christopher Mooney, "Education's Prism," *Cross Currents* 38 (Winter 1988–89): 397.

10. Elizabeth Minnich, "The Future of Civic Education" (Address to AAC conference on "Collegiate Education and the Cultivation of Civic Consciousness," Chicago, Ill., 13 April 1991), 1.

11. Suzanne W. Morse, *Renewing Civic Capacity*, ASHE-ERIC Reports #8 (Washington: American Society for Higher Education, 1989), 7.

12. To see this shift in the perspective on leadership one need only look at some of the most significant and frequently cited books on leadership in recent years. See, for example, Robert K. Greenleaf, *Servant Leadership* (Ramsey, N.J.: Paulist Press, 1977); James MacGregor Burns, *Leadership* (New York: Harper & Row, 1979); and John W. Gardner, *On Leadership* (New York: Free Press, 1990).

13. Morse, *Renewing Civic Capacity*, 31 and 41. The fact that these concerns have been voiced before, however, does not in any way lessen their importance.

14. Creating an understanding of and appreciation for this concept is a specific goal of Susan Ostrander's teaching about philanthropy. A wonderful illustration of this concept may be found in Dr. Ostrander's address on "The Goals of Liberal Education and the Study of Philanthropy and Voluntarism" (AAC conference on "Collegiate Education and the Cultivation of Civic Consciousness," Chicago, Ill., 12 April 1991).

15. The Platonic and Aristotelean traditions differ on the precise definition of "the good life" (and of "the good") and its essential qualities, but the general perspective outlined here—with the focus on moral and aesthetic excellence—is at the core of both versions of these classical ideals for human existence. For a fuller explanation of these concepts see Aristotle's *Nicomachean Ethics* and Plato's *Republic*.

16. *The Challenge of Connecting Learning* (Washington: Association of American Colleges, 1991), 14.

17. *Ibid.*, 16.

Chapter 3. Teaching About Philanthropy and Voluntarism

18. This is Robert Payton's definition of philanthropy, found in his book *Philanthropy: Voluntary Action for the Public Good* (New York: Macmillan, 1988).

19. See especially Parker Palmer's book *To Know as We Are Known* (San Francisco: Harper & Row, 1983).

20. In 1989, as part of another project, AAC conducted a survey of almost twelve hundred students in twelve arts and sciences fields in thirty-seven four-year institutions of all types. This was not a scientifically selected sample but did include a broad range of students and institutions. The survey was conducted to elicit information about the structure and character of different "majors" or "programs of study-in-depth" and students' experiences in them.

21. In our interviews (see next note), students repeatedly emphasized their appreciation for the interdisciplinary character of the offerings. A significant number of these students said the chance to be involved in some interdisciplinary work was an important factor in their choosing to take one of these courses.

22. All of the student comments in this monograph derive from interviews conducted as part of the extensive evaluation of AAC's Program on Studying Philanthropy. As part of that evaluation, the author spent several days on the

campus of each participating institution talking with the course designers and teachers, other faculty members and administrators, and students who had taken and were then taking these courses. The interviews with students were sometimes conducted in small groups, sometimes one-on-one. In all cases, students were assured that any comments they made would be held in confidence, if they wished; students seemed to feel free to offer both positive and negative opinions about the courses and their experiences in them.

23. In the survey of students in twelve arts and sciences fields cited previously (see note 21 above), only in English, philosophy, and women's studies did a majority of students say it was "usually true" that "course materials and assignments connected to personally significant questions." In only five of the twelve fields (the three above plus sociology and interdisciplinary studies) did a majority say it was "usually true" that "important questions of values and ethics were explored" in their courses. Perhaps most telling were the surprising number of comments students added to their survey forms expressing astonishment that anyone would expect such connections with "real life" questions to be made in a classroom.

24. *Integrity in the College Curriculum* (Washington: Association of American Colleges, 1985), 21.

25. Palmer, *To Know as We Are Known*, 7.

26. Minnich, "The Future of Civic Education in Colleges and Universities," 16.

27. There is a host of psychology and education literature available verifying this point and illustrating how this process works. See the section of the bibliography in Appendix A on "Integrating

Service or Work Experience with Course Work and Academic Learning."

28. We have cited before the results of our survey of students in these courses, Independent Sector's surveys, and others. See note 2.

29. The readings and lectures in another course developed through AAC's Program on Philanthropy provided an overview of the development and dynamics of the nonprofit sector in the American political economy and then raised key questions about the ways in which the structure of nonprofit organizations and the nonprofit sector helps or hinders them in serving "the public good." The course also required students to experience those structures and organizations by working in one for some time. The importance of this latter element was indicated in the comments of students who—echoing sentiments often heard in other courses—said things like, "The experience of volunteering was crucial. Without it the course would have just been too theoretical," or, "The experience in the field made the things we talked about in class 'real'; it made them make sense."

30. Richard Morrill, "Educating for Democratic Values," *Liberal Education* 68 (September/October 1982): 365.

31. Of the students responding to the survey, at least 68 percent said they were more likely to get involved, stay involved, or increase their participation in voluntary activities as a result of what they learned in these courses. This trend was even more pronounced for those in courses that included an experiential component. (For a fuller presentation and explanation of the survey results on these points, see Appendix D.)

Chapter 4. Courses, Dynamics, Students, and Outcomes

32. The selection of proposals to be funded was made with help of a Project Advisory Committee composed of experts in the field. The members of this committee are listed in the Introduction on page xiii.

33. A full list of these courses appears in Appendix C. Two institutions that received grants—Harvard University and Southern University—dropped out of the program when various local circumstances made it impossible for them to proceed with their course offerings as specified under the terms of the grant.

34. We first heard this description from Robert Payton, who borrowed and paraphrased it from some work of the anthropologist Clifford Geertz.

35. Mary Oates' own description of the course and its purposes, quoted in *Liberal Education* 74 (September/October 1988): 34.

36. For an explanation of the source and methodology related to students' comments, see note 23.

37. From an interview with Robert Klaus, instructor of this course; quoted in *Liberal Education* 74 (September/October 1988): 33.

38. From Mike Martin's syllabus for "A Life of Service" for the academic year 1989–90.

39. From an interview with Robert Hunt; quoted in *Liberal Education* 74 (September/October 1988): 32.

40. From an interview with Ronnie Steinberg; quoted in *Liberal Education* 75 (September/October 1989): 33.

41. From the syllabus for "Philanthropy and Community" for the 1990–91 academic year.

Chapter 5. Insights and Opportunities

42. See note 2.

43. In some fieldwork programs and courses, the surrounding community comes to be exploited as a laboratory for the college's use and convenience. Many service agencies are cautious after bad experiences with student volunteers. The Wingspread publication "Principles of Good Practice for Combining Service and Learning" provides an extremely helpful set of suggestions and guidelines for how to set up such programs. (See the Selected Resources in Appendix B.)

44. At nine of the fourteen institutions participating in the AAC/AAFRC project, senior administrators said that the courses highlighted or symbolized the institution's commitment to do more with voluntary and community service—one of the reasons they were pleased to have the course in the curriculum.

45. *Challenge of Connecting Learning*, 13.

46. For an extraordinarily helpful summary of the research on the problems with conventional modes of teaching in our schools and the potential value of experience in teaching and learning, see Lauren Resnick, "Learning In and Out of School," *Educational Researcher* 16 (December 1987): 13–20.

47. David Kolb's book, *Experiential Learning: Experience as A Source of Learning and Development* (Englewood Cliffs, N.J.: Prentice Hall, 1984) is widely available. An unpublished copy of Fred Emery's very useful paper "Educational Paradigms: An Epistemological Revolution" (1980) was provided by Tim Stanton, Associate Director of Stanford University's Haas Center for Public Service.